EXPERIMENTS

WITH

LIGHT

by the Authors

Nelson F. Beeler
and Franklyn M. Branley

EXPERIMENTS

WITH

LIGHT

Illustrated by Anne Marie Jauss

71993

Thomas Y. Crowell Company:
New York

Manufactured in the United States of America
by the Vail-Ballou Press, Inc., Binghamton, New York

LIBRARY OF CONGRESS CATALOG CARD No. 58-5591

Sixth Printing

Dedicated to
pioneers of the past,
whose efforts have brought us
closer to truth, and to
pioneers of the future,
who will probe new frontiers
of knowledge

Contents

EXPERIMENTS

WITH

LIGHT

CHAPTER 1

LIGHT TRAVELS IN THE DARK

THE WAKING hours of all of us are spent in light, either artificial or daylight. But while we are consciously aware of lights and lighted objects, the light energy itself is actually invisible. When we look at a source of light (the sun or the stars, a candle or a match) or when we look at an object that reflects light (the moon, the planets, an illuminated wall, or the pages of this book), we get the sensation of light registered by our brain.

Sunlight illuminates the earth brightly, yet the space through which it travels from the sun to the earth is lightless—dark. For in space there is nothing to reflect light, no dust particles or bits of water vapor. Space is empty, a vacuum.

The room that you are sitting in as you read this book

is filled with radio waves from all the stations in the world. You are not aware of them because you are not equipped to receive them. But if you had a sensitive radio set, an instrument which can receive this particular form of radiant energy, you could tune in any of the waves that you pleased. The radio set would turn the radiant energy into sound which our brain could detect.

Like radio waves, sun energy flooding through the windows cannot be seen as it moves across a room. But if that energy hits the eye directly, or reflects back from dust particles or some object in the room, the eye, like the radio, *tunes in* the energy and it registers on our brain as the sensation of sight.

You can prove that light travels in the dark by means of a curved glass towel bar from the bathroom. Some towel bars are easily detached by merely sliding them out of their two holders which are fixed to the wall. Cut a hole in the center of a piece of black construction paper, or carbon paper—a hole just large enough so that either end of the towel bar can be pushed through. Go into a darkened room and hold this end of the bar against a lighted flashlight. Fold the black paper around the flashlight so that all the light is masked except that which enters the end of the glass bar. You will see that the straight portion of the transparent bar is not visible.

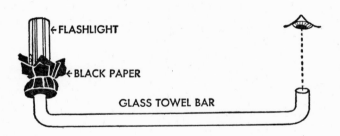

FLASHLIGHT

BLACK PAPER

GLASS TOWEL BAR

Now look at the other end of the bar. It appears brightly lighted. Light energy streams out of this end, hits the eye, and is registered as visible light. But the energy going through the straight part of the glass is moving *in the dark.* The light gets around the corners of the towel bar by reflecting from the inside surfaces of the glass. The angles of reflection are such that very little light gets out until it reaches the end surface of the towel bar.

You can make an interesting house number sign that works because of this same principle: that light is visible only when it is reflected from a surface. Make a box 7 inches long and 4 inches square on the ends. (The sizes given here are approximate. You may use any available box that has these proportionate dimensions. A wooden chalk box would do very well, or any other box of similar size.) On the inside of one end of the box, and closer to the bottom than to the top, screw a standard electric bulb receptacle. Attach wires to this receptacle, as follows: loosen the bolts, twist the bared wire around each bolt,

3

and tighten. Bore a small hole in the box at the same end and run the wires through. Then attach an electric plug to the end of the wires. Fasten a small strip of wood along each inside end of the box, about 1 inch from the top.

To make the top, cut 2 pieces of wood the same length as the box, but smaller enough in width to allow for a slit between them, along the middle length of the box. The slit should only be wide enough to admit the glass plate that you will use for your sign.

You may use ordinary window glass. Double-weight glass would be better. Plate glass would be best. If your box measures 4 by 7 inches, have your hardware dealer cut a piece of glass 5 inches wide and 6½ inches long. (No matter what size box you are using, the glass should be 5 inches in width and ½ inch shorter than the box is long.)

Place (do not glue) pieces of gummed paper tape on the glass so that they cover the entire surface, except for a narrow margin at the top edge and both side edges. Draw the numbers of your house in the center of the gummed paper, and then cut them out carefully. Arrange the strips on the glass so that the margins are straight, and then glue the strips to the glass.

Now we are going to etch the numbers and a border onto the glass. This can be done with a piece of emery cloth and some valve-grinding compound. You can get the

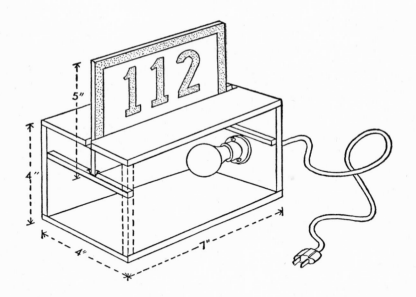

cloth at a hardware store, and the compound at either a garage or an auto supply store. Place a small amount of the compound on the exposed sections of the glass, and then rub the compound back and forth with some of the emery cloth. Try to keep the abrasive away from the paper as much as possible, but don't be alarmed if the paper wears away a little, as this will give the edges of the numbers a soft effect. When you have rubbed the figures and the border until they are rough and look frosty, remove the paper. You are now ready to assemble the sign.

Put one of the top sections in place and then, resting the glass on the wooden strips at the ends of the box, set and hold the glass upright against the top section, as shown in the diagram. On both of the wooden strips mark with a pencil the edges of the glass. Remove the glass and the top section, and put small brads in the wooden strips at the pencil marks, to hold the glass securely in place.

Now nail down one of the top sections, put the glass in position, and nail down the other top section. Seal the spaces around the glass and any other parts of the box where there might be light leaks. (This can be done with plastic wood, water putty, or plain glazier's putty.) Put a 10-watt bulb in the socket and plug in the light cord to an electric outlet. The numerals and border will light up brightly while the rest of the glass plate will be invisible. If you line the box with aluminum foil this will increase the light which passes through the glass and will make the letters glow more brightly.

If you wish to use this sign outdoors, it must be water-proofed. This you can do by sealing the box thoroughly with putty, painting it, and then covering the paint with two coats of spar varnish. The light cord must be of heavy weight for outside use, and the connections must be well covered and protected with tape. (Caution: Do not use a bulb any brighter than 10 watts. A larger bulb will generate too much heat, which cannot escape.) Because they can be easily read at night and are attractive, these signs

6

are often used outside doctors' offices, tourist homes, or similar places.

Now, let's see why the sign works. Light travels in the dark. It goes right through the glass because there is nothing to reflect it. But when it strikes the numbers and the border, the frosted roughened sections, it reflects from that surface to the eye, and thus becomes visible light. The numbers and border appear to glow as though they were giving out a light of their own. Likewise any flaw in the glass, such as an air bubble, will reflect light and become visible.

Another easy way to show that light travels in the dark is seen in the next illustration. Coat the inside of a cardboard carton with black paper by pasting black paper to it; or paint the inside with black paint, which will give a dull surface (for example, water color). Cut holes in each of the ends of the box. The holes should be exactly opposite each other and just large enough to let a cardboard tube fit snugly.

The tubes should be 4-inch lengths cut from a roll of kitchen paper towels, or they may be mailing tubes. Paint or cover the inside of the tubes with black, too. Put tape around the places where the tubes enter the box.

Cover all cracks in the box with paper tape. Put a cardboard cover on the box. This should be painted black on

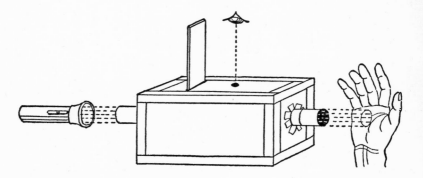

its under side, too. Tape the cover securely. It is essential that no light from outside get into the box.

With a sharp knife, cut a ½-inch peephole in the top of the box. Now shine a bright flashlight into one of the tubes. The light will pass through the box. You can prove it by holding your hand near the opening of the tube across from the flashlight.

Peep into the box while the light is traveling through it. It will be completely dark in the box in spite of the fact that the "light" is passing through it. This is easier to explain if you say that radiant energy is passing through the box. This radiant energy strikes the hand and is reflected to your eye. We are not aware of this radiant energy unless it strikes the eye and the eye reports the fact to the brain.

Let a little smoke from a blown-out match into the box through one of the tubes. You will see a beam passing

8

through the smoke. You can see this because the particles of smoke bounce some of the radiant energy up to your eye. Slip a long card through a slit in the top of the box. As soon as the card hits the area through which the radiant energy is passing, the card becomes lighted and we can see it.

It is often inconvenient to use the words "radiant energy" in place of "light." On the other hand, unless we separate the two ideas much confusion results. In the rest of this book, whenever you run across the word "light," be sure you know which meaning you should give the word. *Light* is sometimes used to mean the radiant *energy* which comes from glowing objects. It is sometimes used to mean the *sensation* of light which our brain produces.

CHAPTER 2

MEASURING LIGHT

MAN'S CONQUEST of the dark, from the days of the smoldering torch to the development of modern electric lighting, is a fascinating chapter in the history of science.

When scientists set out to study light, the first thing they had to do was to find a way to measure it. Because the chief source of illumination at that time was the candle, scientists used it as a unit and measured light in terms of candle power. The term candle power is still in use although better standards of measurement are now available. Scientists say that a lamp is as bright as a certain number of candles would be if they were burning in the same place. The candle power of a light is the measure of the brightness of the light at its source.

The amount of light that strikes this page is called the

illumination. And in order to measure this illumination we must consider not only the brightness of the source of the light, but also how far away this page is from the source. If we measure the distance of the page from the light in terms of feet, and the brightness of the light in terms of candles, we express the illumination in terms of foot candles. One foot candle is the amount of illumination that we would get on this page from a candle burning 1 foot away.

To get an even better idea of how light is measured, we can make a light meter, or photometer. For this we will need two flat pieces of paraffin and a piece of metal foil from a candy bar. (Use the kind of paraffin that comes in flat slabs in a 1-pound box.) Place the unwrinkled metal foil between the two pieces of paraffin and seal it firmly by heating the edges of the paraffin with a match so that they will melt slightly.

For the frame of the photometer, you can use the box that the paraffin came in. (Or you can substitute a butter or oleomargarine box the same size.) Cut an opening the size of a dime in the center of one of the long sides of the box. Place the paraffin unit in the box so that the foil between the two slabs falls along the diameter of the hole. Then cut a hole the size of a half dollar in each end of the box, and set it up as shown in the diagram.

11

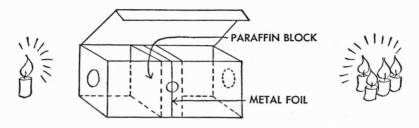

PARAFFIN BLOCK

METAL FOIL

You can improve the photometer by coating the inside of the box with black ink. However, if you are using a waxed butter box, it is easier and just as effective to line the box with a piece of black construction or carbon paper. This helps to absorb reflections from the paraffin, and keeps stray beams of light from affecting the measurement.

It is best to do the following experiment at night or in a room which can be completely darkened. Cut down a number of candles so that when they are lit the flame will be on a line with the openings in the ends of the box. (Or you can raise the meter box by setting it on books or blocks of wood.) Place one candle on each side of the box, about 1 foot away and on a line with each end hole. Now look at your paraffin unit through the dime-sized hole on the front of the box. If the box is not exactly halfway between the 2 lighted candles, the 2 paraffin pieces will not be equally bright. Move one of the candles either closer to or farther away from the box, until both pieces of paraffin are of equal brightness. Notice that, if the candles are giving the same amount of light, they will now be an equal distance from the metal foil.

Now place 4 candle stubs on one side of the light meter and a single one on the other side. Move the meter box and the one candle to a position where, looking through the dime-sized hole, both pieces of paraffin are equally bright. Measure the distance to the candles from the foil between the paraffin pieces. You will find that the four candles are about twice as far from the meter as is the single candle. In other words, light twice as far away must be 4 times (or 2 times 2) as bright if it is to give the same illumination.

If you have plenty of candle ends, try 9 candles against 1, and measure the distances from the meter to the source of light again. You can use small birthday candles for this, but if you do, be sure to use birthday candles on both sides of the meter. This time you will find that the 9 candles are 3 times as far away as is the single candle when both pieces of paraffin are equally bright. In other words, a source 3 times as far away must be 9 (or 3 times 3) times as bright if the illumination is to be equal at the meter.

This light meter demonstrates a basic law of light. To double illumination, we need 4 times as much candle power at the source; to triple illumination, the source must be 9 times as bright. This law of physics is a good one to remember when you are reading, studying, or doing close work of any sort. Be sure to use a light bulb that gives plenty of light. It follows also that if you move twice as far away from a light, you will be getting only ¼ as much illumination. And if you move 3 times as far away, you will get only ⅑ as much. Even the proper-sized bulb becomes valueless if you are too far away from it when you are reading.

You can make another type of light meter by following a principle discovered over a hundred years ago by Robert Bunsen, a German chemist.

Cut a piece of white typing paper in half. Rub a small bit of butter on the center of the paper, to make a grease spot the size of a quarter. You need rub the butter only on one side. Stand the paper upright between two books. Then place a lighted candle about a foot in front of the paper. When you turn out all the lights, the paper will appear white because it reflects light back to the eye. The spot will appear dark because it lets through much of the candlelight that falls on it. Now set up a second candle on the other side of the paper. When both candles are the same distance away from the paper, the grease spot will disappear and the paper will be evenly lighted.

You can make a still more elaborate photometer based

14

on the same principle. Cut a piece of paper the same size as the end of a butter carton. Make a quarter-sized grease spot on the center of the paper. Fasten the paper upright at the center of the box. (It may be held in position with strips of Scotch Tape.) Cut a hole the size of a quarter in the center of each end of the carton, making sure each hole is in line with the grease spot. Cut out a hole the size of a half dollar in the center of the carton cover, making sure that the edge of the paper that contains the grease spot falls along the diameter of the hole.

Cut a cube 2 inches on each side from a piece of wood. Draw a diagonal on one face of the cube. Saw the cube in half along this diagonal line. This will make 2 solid wood pieces, called prisms, each having a triangle for top and bottom. Glue small pocket mirrors (they should be the same size) to the sawed faces of these prisms and place them in the carton as shown in the illustration here.

Go into a darkened room and place candles on both

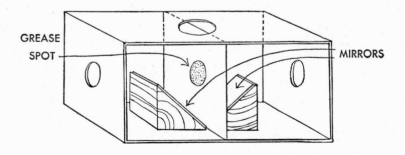

GREASE SPOT · MIRRORS

sides of the box, so that light enters the photometer through the side holes. Look through the large hole in the front of the box. You will see a reflection from each side of the grease spot. When both sides of the grease spot have the same illumination, the reflections will appear equally bright. It is easy to detect a small difference in illumination with this instrument.

Still another effective light meter can be made by using plaster of Paris. First remove the top from a 1-pound butter box. Measure off 2¾ inches on the long side of the box and draw a line down the side at this point. Then cut a small slot along this line. Cut another slot in the nearest diagonal corner. From the top of the box cut a piece that is 1 inch longer than necessary to form a diagonal from the slotted corner to the slotted line. Cut ¼-inch tongues in each end of this piece, and fit these tongues into the slots as shown in the diagram, taking care that the partition fits snugly and securely.

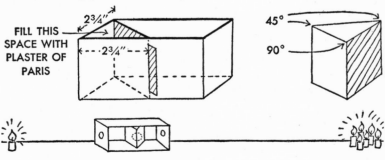

FILL THIS SPACE WITH PLASTER OF PARIS

2¾"

2¾"

45°

90°

Now you are ready to mix your plaster of Paris. Put about a half pint of water in a shallow bowl. Sift in the powdered plaster of Paris until two small islands form. Do not stir the mixture until the *two* islands form. Now stir the mixture carefully so that you do not fold too much air into the plaster.

Bounce the bowl a couple of times on a folded dish towel. This is to remove any air bubbles which may have been trapped in the plaster during the stirring. Without further stirring, pour the mixture into the triangular section you have made in the carton.

Let the plaster of Paris set for at least 24 hours. After it has hardened, remove the carton and you will have a kind of wedge of plaster called a triangular prism. The prism will have two triangles for top and bottom. The triangles will have one 90-degree angle and two 45-degree angles.

To use this prism as a light meter substitute it for the paraffin slabs in the first box you used. Stand the prism on one of its triangular faces. Place the long side of the triangle along the back of the box.

Place the edge of the prism so that it is opposite the mid-line of the hole in the front of the box. Now as you look through the hole, you will see two slanting faces of the prism. If one face has more illumination than the other, they will appear to meet at a sharp line. When the faces of the prism have equal illumination, the line between them disappears. This meter is used in the same way you used the paraffin slab meter.

Much progress has been made in the study of light over the past hundred years, despite the fact that the early scientists had to base their findings on rough measurements made with meters similar to the ones described here.

Today, however, light is measured much more precisely by the use of electronic light meters. These are sensitive instruments that change tiny amounts of light energy into small electric currents. The current flowing through the instrument moves a pointer across a dial. The dial is marked in units of illumination. With this kind of meter a scientist can determine more precisely the amount of illumination that is falling on a surface. Portable light meters which work on this principle are very handy for photographers who need to know the amount of illumination on any object they want to photograph. Without the meter, the camera fan has to guess at the amount of illumination. The light meter gives more precise information and the photographer is more likely to get a good picture every time.

CHAPTER 3

THE NATURE OF LIGHT

How DO WE see things? Some of the ancient Greeks had an interesting explanation. They believed that all objects, whether houses, trees, or animals sprayed out small images of themselves in all directions. When one of these images entered the eye of a person, he "saw" the object. According to this theory, objects apparently shut off the spray of images when darkness falls since we cannot see things in the dark.

The Greeks made no attempt to test this idea. The explanation sounded reasonable to them and they resisted anyone who tried to show that it might be wrong. A more dependable knowledge of the nature of the world has been built up in the past two centuries mainly because scientists have used a different attack upon their problems. One of the ways used to attack a problem is to first make a good guess as to what is happening and then test the guess to see if it comes near to explaining what is going on.

For example, a modern scientist might wonder how light travels from an object to his eye. To find the answer he would first study the facts about light which are known and, on the basis of these facts, would propose a guess, or hypothesis, which might explain the facts.

Let's say that he proposes the hypothesis that light travels in straight streams of small packets which are something like small bullets. The hypothesis is probably sound if it will explain every sort of light phenomenon that can be encountered. He will then proceed to test the hypothesis, which means that he will try to see if it can explain the things that happen to light.

The kind of thinking used to test a hypothesis is sometimes called "if-then" reasoning. For example, the scientist might reason that *if* light is composed of little particles which are moving rapidly in a straight line, *then* solid objects placed in a beam of light should cast sharp-edged shadows. The "bullets" which strike the object should be stopped, but the ones that just graze the edge of the object should go zipping past. Where they land there should be light, and where they do not strike, there should be darkness. Scientists observed that this is indeed the case, and the bullet hypothesis was thereby supported.

But a scientist does not conclude that any hypothesis is the true answer simply because one bit of evidence is found that supports it. His hypothesis must be tested in many other ways before he can be sure. Merely supporting a hypothesis and actually proving that it is the only true explanation are quite different.

Suppose that you intend to test further the hypothesis that light travels in straight streams of small packets that are like small bullets. You could reason like this: *If* light does travel in this way, *then* it should travel through a series of fine slits and come out the other side unchanged. A collection of slits, each separated from the other by a thin line of solid material, is called a grating. It is usually called a diffraction grating for reasons which we shall see.

Let's make a diffraction grating and test the straight stream of small packets hypothesis. Coat a piece of window glass 3 by 4 inches in size with black India ink. It is well to clean the glass carefully first with detergent to remove all grease so that the ink will stick to the glass. Use a fine brush to get an even coating over the entire surface. When the ink has dried thoroughly, place the glass on a flat surface and, using a sharp sewing needle, draw a series of parallel lines as close together as you can through the coating of ink, exposing the glass. A ruler with a metal edge is best for getting really straight lines and sharp clean cuts through the ink. Try not to scratch the glass. Bear down only enough to remove the dry ink. Start ½ inch from one edge of the glass and draw one line after the other until you have covered an area about an inch wide. This series of clear and black spaces is the grating.

Gratings used in a science laboratory may have 30,000 lines to the inch but these require expensive equipment to make. You will be doing well if you are able to get 50 lines to the inch on your grating.

Cut a slit about 2 inches long and about as wide as a pencil lead in a piece of heavy paper the size of a postcard. Use a single-edge razor blade to make the edges of the slit clean and not fuzzy. Make the cuts exactly parallel.

Set up a lighted unshaded lamp bulb 8 feet away. Stand facing the bulb. Hold the slitted card at arm's

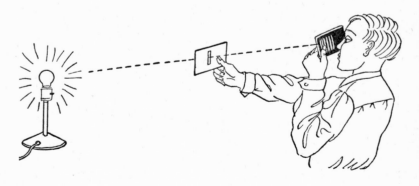

length. Hold the grating directly in front of your eye. Look through the grating with one eye at the light coming through the slit. The eye which is not looking through the grating will be shielded from the light by the unscratched coating of India ink on the glass, so you can keep both eyes open during the observations.

Line up the brightly lighted slit with the lines of the grating. You will see an image of the slit, but the image will be rimmed with a spectrum containing all the colors of the rainbow. When white light is spread out into a spectrum this way, it is said to be diffracted. This accounts for the term diffraction grating.

Now *if* light were really made of tiny bullets, *then* you should see only a sharp, bright image of the slit, because the bullets which get through the opening would continue in their straight path to your eye. They could not bend off to the side to form a fuzzy pattern. The spectrum which appears on each side of the slit cannot be explained by the hypothesis. It looks as though our idea is not entirely acceptable. We will have to admit that the evidence does not support the hypothesis.

When scientists were confronted with this evidence, they proposed another hypothesis to explain it. They said that maybe light really travels in waves, like ripples on a pond. Let's test this hypothesis by "if-then" reasoning.

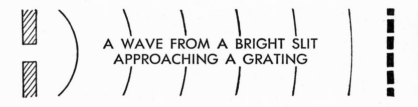

A WAVE FROM A BRIGHT SLIT
APPROACHING A GRATING

If light is moving in waves after it leaves the slit, *then* a wave should reach the glass and start through the grating. (See the illustration here.) Let's say that the first part of the wave to meet the grating goes through a clear space. It would then come out on the other side of the space as a tiny wavelet. As the rest of the wave arrived at the grating, each clear space between the inked lines would also serve as a starting point for a tiny new wave which would start up on the other side of the space. This tiny wave, or wavelet, would spread out on either side of the opening. Note, however, that the foremost part of the wave meets the center opening of the grating before the rest of the wave reaches the side openings. Therefore the wavelet which gets through the center space has time to spread out a little before the other parts of the wave get up to the glass and through their openings in the grating.

Upon coming out on the other side of the grating, these tiny wavelets merge into a new wave which bends to the right and left of the center line of the grating. They should

24

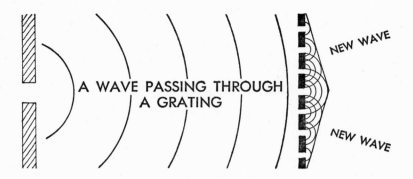

A WAVE PASSING THROUGH A GRATING

NEW WAVE

NEW WAVE

appear to fan out. We have seen that these waves continue. At a little distance from the grating they enter the eye and produce the impression that the light is coming from the slit in a fan-shaped pattern.

If we suppose further that the wave of incoming white light is really a collection of little wavelets of different colors, some wavelets, say the red ones, should be bent more than the blues or violets when they pass through the openings and set up their new wavelet series. These colored light waves on fanning out should produce a spectrum at either side of the slit. This is exactly what we observe. The wave hypothesis seems to be supported— at least in this instance.

Look through the grating at the slit again. Notice the appearance of the slit carefully. It appears to have a series of fine lines drawn through it vertically. Let's see if the wave hypothesis can account for these lines.

If light moves in a continuous wave, *then* one part of the wave should come through the middle of the slit without being bent at all. This part of the wave should go through the grating and form wavelets. The new wavelets should overlap each other on the eye side of the grating and form a new wave.

But this new wave should have some places where the wavelets strengthen each other. These places should appear bright. The new wave should have other places along it where the wavelets cancel each other. These places should appear dark. There should be a series of bright lines and dark lines apparently coming from the slit. This is exactly what we see. The wave theory can account for the appearance of the black lines in the image of the slit.

You can see these same fine lines if you peep at a distant bright light through a slit made by holding two of your fingers very close together but not touching. You can see them at a place where light comes through the small opening between doors which do not quite touch when they are closed.

Some further evidence in support of the wave theory can be obtained from a grating ruled on a shiny metal mirror. The spectrum is then produced when light reflects from the ridges of the scratches. A phonograph record is a reasonably good grating of this sort.

Stand facing the sun or a brightly lighted lamp. Hold a phonograph record (preferably a microgrooved record) close to your eye and parallel to the floor. Look over the edge of the record at the reflection of the sun or of the lamp where it strikes the grooved part of the record. You can see objects reflected in the record but they all appear to have a fringe of colors about them. Here the light, instead of moving through slits, is being reflected from the tops of the ridges on the plastic disk. The presence of the color fringes again supports the wave hypothesis.

The colors that you see in mother-of-pearl are due to this "grating effect." The oyster or clam makes its shell by depositing layer upon layer of lime. The edges of these layers make a grating which serves as a reflecting surface for light. Mother-of-pearl buttons are made by stamping out disks from clam shells. You can duplicate these wonderful colors on wax if you proceed carefully.

Get a large mother-of-pearl button which shows a good play of colors and borrow from the kitchen a square of paraffin, the kind used to cover jars of jelly. Place the button face down on one side of the paraffin and put a piece of thin wood or metal on the other side. Secure the combination in a vise or hold it between pliers and press the button slowly but firmly into the wax. Remove the button and examine the indentation it has made.

Colors appear on the wax because it is now a copy of the grating on the shell. But they appear only when you look at the wax under a lamp. Try several positions to get the correct angle at which the light is broken up most completely into its spectrum. The colors observed in mother-of-pearl are due, therefore, to the form of the material and not to a chemical pigment or dye. Thus the hypothesis that light travels in waves is bolstered by another piece of evidence from an unexpected source.

It should be apparent from these experiments that the wave theory is useful for explaining *some* kinds of light phenomena. The bullet theory is useful for explaining some *other* kinds of light phenomena. Note that we can still call ourselves scientific and not know the final answer to the problem we originally started out to solve. We use ideas to attack problems by "if-then" reasoning, but we stand ready to change our ideas when new evidence is presented. Scientists who believe in the bullet theory do not go out and beat up those who believe in the wave theory. Scientists use what is useful in both theories.

Perhaps one of you who reads this book will propose a theory one day which will explain how light *really* works under all conditions. Until then we must use the bullet theory to explain how light does some things, and the wave theory to explain how light does other things.

CHAPTER 4

MEASURING THE SPEED OF LIGHT

THE ANCIENTS did not believe that light took time to travel from the source to the thing which was being lighted. They felt that as soon as a torch was lighted, objects even at great distances were immediately lighted by it. This is not so odd because it is difficult to think of the speed of light. We joke about the fellow who was so fast that he could blow out the lamp and get into bed before the room was dark.

We still do not know how fast light travels even though men have been trying to find the answer for almost three hundred years. We have come close to the answer but we do not know what the true speed is. All measurements are only as good as the instruments used to make the measurements. As men have made better instruments, they have been able to come closer to the correct answer.

One of the interesting aspects of scientific investigations is finding ways of measuring things which have not been measured before. The first man to get a fairly accurate measurement of the speed of light was Ole Roemer, a Danish astronomer. He thought up a clever scheme for doing this while he was working in Paris in 1675, a hundred years before the American Revolution. The measurement is very close to the speed of light as it is accepted today, despite the fact that he was working before many of the modern instruments of measurement had been invented.

Roemer observed the moons of the planet Jupiter through his telescope. As the moons moved around the planet, they could be seen to disappear in back of it. The moons are said to be eclipsed by the planet when this happens. Since any particular moon moves in an orderly way, it must be eclipsed at regular intervals. Roemer calculated just how long the interval should be between eclipses of the nearest moon to the planet.

However, when Roemer timed the moon he found that it was not eclipsed according to his prediction. In fact, the difference between an observation made in June and one made in December amounted to about one thousand seconds. The earth is closest to Jupiter in June (*E* in the

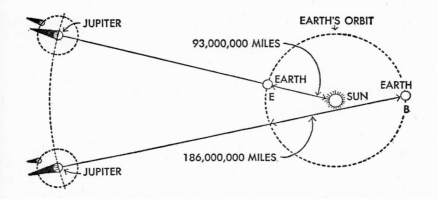

diagram). Then the eclipses occurred every 42.5 hours. The earth is at its farthest point from Jupiter in December (*B* in the diagram). In December the eclipses occurred every 42.5 hours plus 1,000 seconds. Roemer explained the difference in this way.

He knew that the distance from the earth to the sun was 93,000,000 miles. The distance across the whole orbit of the earth (*EB* on the diagram) then is twice this, or 186,000,000 miles. The 1,000 seconds must be used up by the light from the moon of Jupiter traveling across the orbit of the earth. If light travels 186,000,000 miles in 1,000 seconds, it must travel 186,000 miles in 1 second. This is an almost unbelievable speed. If light could bend by itself, a ray of light would go 7½ times around the world in 1 second. It is no wonder that the ancients thought that light moved in no time at all.

31

Roemer was ridiculed by many for making such a non-sensical statement, for it was obvious, said the people of his day, that nothing could travel so fast. But there were men of science who believed that he was right. For decades they attempted to find a way of measuring the velocity of light by using distances on earth, because earth distances could be measured more accurately than the distance to the sun. And they would not have to wait the 6 months between June and December to get the difference between times of eclipses.

But more than a hundred and fifty years elapsed before the first laboratory measurement of the speed of light was made. Before Roemer's time one of the big problems that made the accurate measuring of the speed of light an impossibility was that man could not measure very small fractions of a second. A Frenchman, Armand Fizeau, solved the problem in 1849. He reflected a strong beam of light from the front face of a clear glass plate held at a 45-degree angle. The light from the plate passed between the cogs of a toothed wheel that was rotated at a measured speed. The light came out the other side of the rotating wheel in a series of flashes. The flashes were sent to a mirror on a mountain about 5 miles away. Light from this mirror was reflected back to the observer who was stationed behind the glass plate and rotating wheel. By

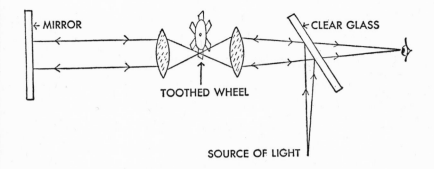

MIRROR

CLEAR GLASS

TOOTHED WHEEL

SOURCE OF LIGHT

changing the speed of the toothed wheel, the observer could block out the light which was returning from the mirror on the mountain by having it fall on the tooth of the wheel, or he could allow it to pass through a space between two teeth.

Fizeau used a wheel with 720 teeth and 720 even spaces between the teeth, making a total of 1,440 sections. When the wheel was rotating about 12 times a second, the reflected light flashes did not get through to the observer. He reasoned that each flash of light must be moving over to the mountain and back in just the time it took for a space in the cogwheel to be replaced by a tooth.

The time needed for a cog to move to a place where an opening had been was 1/18,144 of a second. During this time light must have traveled about 10 miles. (Fizeau had measured the distance as 17,266 meters). The speed of light by this method appeared to be 195,000 miles a second. We know now that this is about 5 per cent faster than actual.

Fizeau's method did not give precise results because there was no way of knowing the precise moment of total blackout. Albert A. Michelson, an American, and his associates were able to get much better results by improving on Fizeau's scheme.

In their plan an 8-sided rotating mirror was substituted for the rotating cogged wheel. As shown in the illustration here, light from a strong source passed through a narrow slit to be reflected by face number 1 of the rotating mirror. The image of the slit was reflected by prism *A* to prism *B* and to the concave mirror at *C*. The light then traveled 22 miles to a mirror located on a mountain top. Mirror *D* reflected the light to mirror *E*. Mirror *E* bounced the light back to *D*, from which it traveled back over the 22 miles to mirror *C* where it was reflected to prism *F*. From *F* the light was reflected to face 5 of the mirror and finally to the observer.

When the 8-sided mirror was at rest, the reflected light could be seen coming from face 5. When the mirror was rotated slowly, the reflected light was dim or blurred. The speed of rotation was increased. When the rotating mirror was moving just fast enough to bring face 4 up into the position previously occupied by face 5 during the time

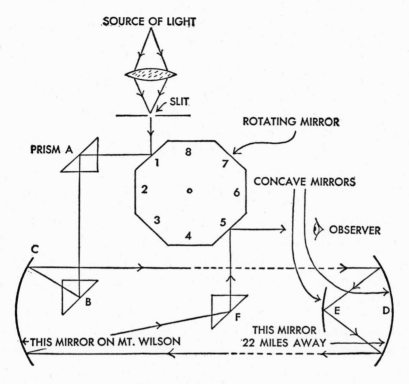

the light was going the 22 miles and back again, the light could be seen being reflected brightly. If the scientist knew how many times a second the rotating mirror was spinning, he could figure how long it took for face 4 to come into the position previously occupied by face 5. He also knew that during this very small interval of time, the light flash had traveled 44 miles through air.

Later Michelson and his fellow workers measured the

speed of light in a vacuum by using a mile-long tube from which all the air was pumped. A 32-sided mirror bounced light back and forth 9 times in this tube by means of a complicated set of mirrors. This work was carried on after Michelson's death in 1931. The speed of light as calculated from these observations was 186,271 miles a second.

Experiments done since 1950 seem to indicate that this speed is still not the true one. Modern methods use radio waves and radar which travel at the speed of light. The rotating mirrors have been replaced by vibrating crystals and electronic devices, which give out flashes much closer together than those coming from the old mirrors. Better methods of measuring short intervals of time have been invented.

Scientists will continue to attempt to get better and better measures of the speed of light. This speed is believed to be the fastest that can be attained in the universe. It is also a necessary part of many calculations which test the Einstein theory of the nature of the universe. Many equations of modern atomic physics use this speed as part of the calculation, including the famous $E = MC^2$ equation which connects the mass of atomic fission material with the amount of energy which can be obtained from it. C in this famous equation is the speed of light.

CHAPTER 5

MEASURING THE
WAVE LENGTH OF LIGHT

ONE OF THE most difficult ideas to grasp about any form of radiant energy is that it moves in waves. The idea becomes more difficult when you realize that the waves are so small that the distance between the top of one wave and the top of the next one is only a few hundred-thousandths of an inch. This distance is called a wave length. It is possible to measure such small distances, and the task is accomplished with a high precision. Certainly distances so small cannot be measured with measuring tools like yardsticks, but you can set up an experiment using only two pieces of window glass that will give you an idea of how such measuring is done.

Ordinary window glass is not entirely flat. Look through

the window of the room you are sitting in. Do you notice that objects outside the window are a little distorted, especially if you look through the glass at an angle? If you are looking through plate glass, the distortion will not be great. If the glass is ordinary window glass, things outside will appear to wiggle as you move your head from side to side.

If two pieces of this uneven window glass are placed upon each other, they will not touch at all points. They will be separated at some places by thin layers of air which may vary from a few ten-thousandths of an inch at their widest points to nothing at all where the pieces of glass are touching.

Imagine a series of radiant energy waves going through a piece of glass and into one of these *layers* of air. For the sake of simplicity in our experiment, let's not worry about what happens within the glass plates themselves. Some of the waves reflect from the first glass surface which is the boundary of the air layer. These waves start back toward our eyes. Some of the waves move through the thin air film and are reflected back from the second glass surface. These waves also move back toward our eye. If the waves arrive moving up and down in step with each other, they will be seen as light. But since the air films are not the same thickness throughout, some waves return out of step with those reflecting from the first glass surface. It is to be expected that the upswing of some of these first waves should occur at the same place as the downswing of the second set. Whenever this happens the two sets of waves cancel each other and we see no light at all.

If light does travel in waves, *then* the illustration here shows what might take place in the air film between two perfectly flat glass plates separated at one edge by a thin piece of tissue paper. This air film is wedge-shaped. It

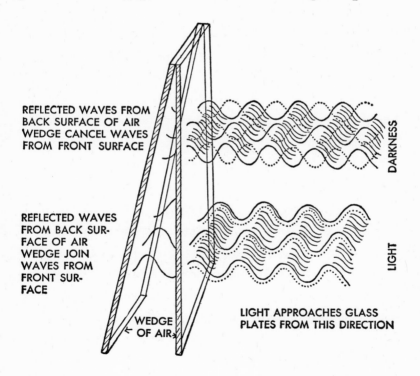

REFLECTED WAVES FROM BACK SURFACE OF AIR WEDGE CANCEL WAVES FROM FRONT SURFACE

DARKNESS

REFLECTED WAVES FROM BACK SURFACE OF AIR WEDGE JOIN WAVES FROM FRONT SURFACE

LIGHT

WEDGE OF AIR

LIGHT APPROACHES GLASS PLATES FROM THIS DIRECTION

starts as a very, very tiny film and increases gradually in thickness. In the drawing the actual size of the film is magnified many thousands of times in order to make the waves large enough to see.

One part of the wedge will be just the right thickness to allow waves to come through in step. At a place just below this, the wedge is thicker. A wave which crosses this particular part of the wedge will be out of step when it bounces back. If light does travel in waves, then we should see a collection of parallel black and bright lines when light falls on such an air film bounded by glass.

Let's see whether this does happen. Get two pieces of plate glass about 3 inches square. Set them up as shown here. Use very thin tissue paper to separate the plates at one end and hold the pair together with rubber bands. Pour a tablespoon of rubbing alcohol on three tablespoons of table salt (sodium chloride) that has been placed in a china dish. Light a match to the alcohol and darken the room completely.

After a short time the flame will take on a definite yellow color. Hold the plates so the image of this yellow flame reflects back to your eye from the glass. The image of the flame appears to be made of alternately black and yellow stripes. The radiant energy coming from the sodium flame is composed of waves that are all the same

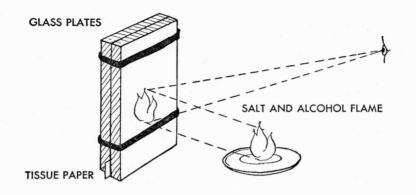

GLASS PLATES

SALT AND ALCOHOL FLAME

TISSUE PAPER

wave length. Scientists can measure the thickness of the paper separating the edges of the glass plates and hence know accurately the dimensions of the wedge-shaped air film between the plates. They can measure the width of the bands of yellow and black which appear on the glass. By using these measurements and doing some calculations, they can determine the distance between the waves (the wave length) of sodium light.

If you have nothing available but window glass, there is no need to use the tissue paper, for plates of window glass are uneven and therefore separated from each other at many points. Hold two pieces of window glass firmly, using the thumb and fingers of each hand, and hold them in the same position as was indicated for the pieces of plate glass. Black and yellow lines will appear but they will not be in parallel rows. Instead, the image will look

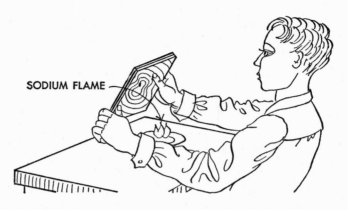

SODIUM FLAME

like a mammoth fingerprint. The yellow and black lines will move to new positions as you squeeze the plates, thus changing the thickness of the air spaces between the two pieces of glass.

Precision lenses are tested by using this idea. From time to time as a lens is being ground, it is placed in a scooped-out hollow in another piece of glass. This hollow has been ground to the exact form of the lens wanted. When no rings of alternate blackness and brightness are seen under sodium light, the lens maker knows that his lens fits the master model perfectly. If it misses fitting by so much as half a wave length of light, the presence of color bands will indicate the fact. Half a wave length of sodium light is about .00001 inch long!

If we had used red light in the previous experiment instead of the yellow sodium light we would have had alternate areas of blackness and of redness; however, the color bands would have been in a different position. Blue light would have produced blue and black bands in an entirely different position on the plate.

What we call white light results from waves of all wave lengths traveling together. In thin soap films like those in a soap bubble, the film is not the same thickness everywhere. When white light falls upon a soap film, therefore, a series of color bands appear in positions on the bubble. These become more clearly defined as the water in the bubble evaporates, making the film thinner and thinner. Also the pull of gravity takes more of the soap to the base of the bubble, making the film thicker there. The film becomes shaped more like a wedge the longer the bubble lasts.

You can prove this by a simple experiment. Blow a soap bubble with a bubble pipe or soda straw and close the end of the pipe with your finger to keep the bubble from going back into the pipe. Let light fall on the bubble from the side. Hold the bubble on the pipe as long as it will last. (A little glycerin added to the soapy water will produce tougher and longer-lasting bubbles.) In a short time bands of color will appear in the upper half of the bubble and the colors will change as the thickness of the film changes.

Many metals combine readily with the oxygen in the air, especially when they are heated. The coating of the metal oxide which is formed is very thin but in most cases it is thick enough to protect the metal from further contact with the air. It is thin enough, however, to allow some light through.

You can see this for yourself. Clean thoroughly a piece of copper foil or wire with sandpaper or emery cloth. You will see the true color of the metal. Then grasp the copper with a pair of pliers and run it through a gas or match flame quickly. The copper will take on a varicolored appearance. This is due to the fact that light is traveling through the different thicknesses of the oxide coating that is formed. Drops of oil which spread out into thin films of varying thickness on puddles in the street produce colors by this same process.

The feathers of many birds and some changeable silks have color because of a thin layer of surface cells. The metallic glint in the feathers of the pigeon and the brilliant colors of the peacock are not due entirely to coloring matter in the feathers but are caused by light passing through thin layers of outside cells. The air film in a cracked piece of ice frequently is just the right thickness and wedge form to produce all the colors of the spectrum.

CHAPTER 6

LIGHT AND COLOR

WE HAVE already found out that radiant energy travels in the dark but that waves of certain length give us the sensation of light when they strike our eyes. We can see objects that are producing light themselves, such as flames, hot filaments, and stars, including our sun. These are called luminous objects. We can also see objects that are reflecting light waves to our eyes, such as the pages of this book, the walls of the room, mountains, fields, buildings, and pavements. These are called illuminated objects.

If you have a chandelier or other lamp which has three-sided glass prisms, remove one of these and hold it so that sunlight falls upon one of the faces. A beautiful spectrum of the colors of sunlight will be formed on the wall or ceiling. This happens because "white" sunlight is made of

45

radiant energy waves of many different wave lengths. Each kind of wave travels at a different speed in glass. Therefore each wave is bent to a different degree when the sunlight passes through the glass of the prism. This variation causes the waves to spread out. After the waves leave the prism and either enter the eye directly or are reflected to the eye from a white surface, we see them as bands of distinct colors.

These colors are usually referred to as red, orange, yellow, green, blue, and violet. It is rather difficult to see each one of these colors distinctly because they blend into one another. Most people see the red, yellow, green, and blue clearly. Recent investigations among a hundred Indian tribes, however, show that some tribes recognize only three colors in the spectrum while others identify as many as eight.

If you do not have a three-sided prism, you can still break sunlight into its spectrum by using a tray of water and a pocket mirror.

Set a square-sided tray near a window through which bright sunlight is streaming. Fill the tray with water to a depth of 1 inch. Lean a pocket mirror in the water on the side of the tray that is farthest from the window, so that sunlight falls upon it after passing through the water. When the mirror is adjusted properly, a spectrum will appear on the upper part of the wall of the room, or upon the ceiling. (The location of the spectrum is determined by the angle at which the rays of the sun are received.) The water wedge made by the mirror and the surface of the water acts as a 3-sided water prism. Perfectly spherical water droplets can break white light up into its many kinds of waves too. This is what causes rainbows.

You have no doubt seen a rainbow in the sky or a spectrum of colors in the spray from a garden hose when sunlight strikes the falling droplets at just the right angle. Have you also noticed that the rainbows you have seen are always in a particular position in the sky? They do not ever appear, for example, directly overhead. They always arch so that the top of the bow is about halfway between the horizon and the point directly overhead. They always appear when the sun is at your back.

The sky behind the rainbow is always hazy or cloudy. This haze or cloud is made of millions upon millions of tiny droplets. Each droplet lets some light waves through it. Each droplet reflects some waves back to the eye, too. (Otherwise, of course, we couldn't see the cloud at all.)

The light which reflects back through the droplets is broken up into the spectrum. From those drops which are at an angle of 42 degrees from our line of sight, only the red rays reach our eyes. The other waves are scattered.

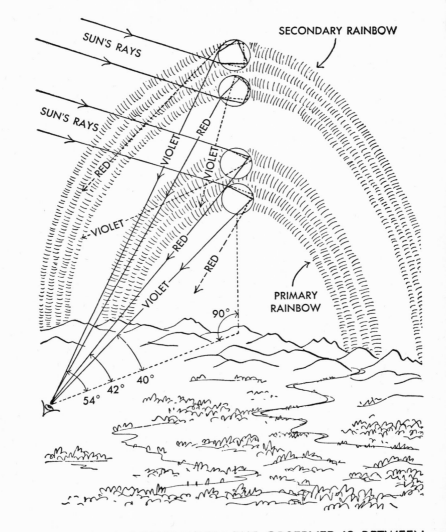

SECONDARY RAINBOW

SUN'S RAYS

SUN'S RAYS

RED

VIOLET

RED

VIOLET

RED

VIOLET

VIOLET

RED

RED

VIOLET

VIOLET

RED

90°

PRIMARY RAINBOW

54° 42° 40°

RAINBOWS OCCUR WHEN THE OBSERVER IS BETWEEN
THE SUN AND DROPLETS IN THE AIR

From droplets 40 degrees from our line of sight violet waves come directly to our eyes. All other waves are scattered.

We can see a rainbow as a band of color between 40 and 42 degrees above the eastern horizon when the sun is just setting at the western horizon. Or above the western horizon when the sun is rising in the east. A second rainbow may sometimes be seen above the first. Such a rainbow is caused by viewing reflected sunlight at a greater angle. This bow will cover a band between 51 and 54 degrees, but the red will be on the lower side of the bow and the violet on top.

Clear window glass lets all the waves of sunlight through. Colored glass absorbs some of the waves and lets only certain ones through. A transparent colored substance like colored cellophane is said to filter the light. A little experimentation with colored cellophane pieces will give you some idea of how light filters work.

You will need pieces of red, green, and blue cellophane. Hold the red piece against the window and look through it. Everything looks red because the red cellophane filters out the blues and greens that are being reflected from objects lighted by the sunlight. Only the waves which produce the sensation of red get through. When you hold the blue piece to the window, the reds and greens are filtered out; and when the green piece is in position, the reds and blues are removed.

If you think of white light approaching the red cellophane and only the red waves getting through, you can see why the cellophane is sometimes said to be red by "subtraction." It is not hard to figure out what should happen if you were to use a piece of red and green cellophane, one on top of the other. Since green cellophane absorbs or subtracts red waves, it sounds reasonable that no light would get through the two pieces. Try it. (It is difficult to get complete blackness with the two pieces of cellophane because each piece is not a complete absorber of all the kinds of waves but one. In other words, the green may let a few of the red waves through; the red may let a few of the green waves through, and so on.)

Most of the colors that we see in objects which reflect light to our eyes result from subtraction. White light falls upon the grass. The grass absorbs red and blue waves and reflects green waves to our eyes. White light falls upon a rose. Green and blue waves are absorbed and the red light is reflected to our eyes. We say that grass is green and a rose is red.

The material which produces the color is called a pigment and is made of molecules just as everything else is. The molecules which go to make up a pigment are of such nature that they can trap some kinds of waves and not others. The colors which are trapped by a certain pigment give the scientist some understanding about what the arrangement of atoms must be like within the molecules of pigment.

If you are now convinced that white light can be broken up into lights of many colors, you are in a position to apply "if-then" reasoning to a new problem. *If* white light is composed of lights of many colors, *then* it should be possible to make white light by mixing the proper kinds of colored lights.

To test this hypothesis you will need three flashlights that produce small spots of light, and pieces of red, blue, and green cellophane. Cover the head of one of the flashlights with three layers of red cellophane that are fastened in place with tape; cover another one in the same manner with three layers of green cellophane, and cover the third one with blue.

Take the flashlights into a dark room and shine the red one on a white screen. Of course you will get a spot of red light. Hold the green flashlight at an equal distance from the screen and shine its light on the spot of red light. The red and green lights will form a spot of yellow light on the screen. When the blue flashlight is directed to the yellow area of the screen, the spot will become almost white. (If

51

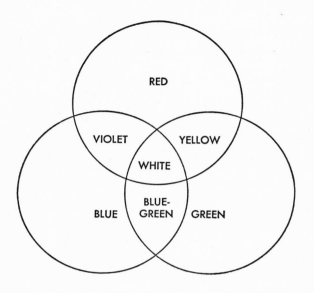

the colors coming through the pieces of cellophane were true spectrum colors, and if they were of the same intensity, the spot of light would be completely white. However it is practically impossible to satisfy these conditions with ordinary equipment.)

In this last experiment you obtained color by addition. Waves in the region of green added to red produced the sensation of yellow, and blue added to yellow produced the sensation we call white. A look at the illustration here shows the various color sensations that result when the three primary or basic colors of light—red, green, and blue—are added together.

There are tens of thousands of different color sensations that you can achieve by addition with a device called a color wheel. To make wheels, cut several 5-inch circles out of cardboard and then mark them off into wedge-shaped sections. Make a number of segments and color them in various combinations. For example, you might divide one of the wheels into 6 segments and color each segment alternately red and green. Use strong bright colors such as poster paints. Put a thumbtack through the center of the disk and then fasten it to the end of a dowel or a round pencil.

Fasten the dowel securely in the chuck of a hand drill and spin the disk while holding it in sunlight or under a bright artificial light. Neither red nor green will be visible, but rather you will see a color that appears more like yellow than like either of the colors that make it up. Try all sorts of combinations to see what color will be produced.

Color wheels such as this work because the eye is receiving several kinds of waves which are following each other in swift succession. The brain is unable to separate one impression from the other, so it places them together. This presents a problem about color which comes about if we are not very careful with the words we use. There is a certain definite wave length of radiant energy which produces the sensation of yellow in our brain. Red waves

53

and green waves, arriving at the eye together, produce this same sensation, yellow, although there are no waves of the yellow wave length in the combination at all.

It is fortunate for those of us whose eyes and brains are equipped to see color that there are such processes as color by addition and subtraction. To the totally color blind there are no greens and yellows, reds and blues. Everything in their world is either black or white, or various shades of gray. Some people, however, are color blind in only a certain range of colors, say red to yellow. They can detect other colors without difficulty.

It is interesting to consider what happens to colors when objects are viewed by the light from a flash of lightning. The white light in this case is extremely intense but of very short duration. The landscape appears to be composed of only blacks, whites, and grays. Apparently the eye requires a little time to react to certain wave lengths and to transmit the proper nerve impulse to the brain for a sensation of color to be formed.

CHAPTER 7

HOW LENSES WORK

PERHAPS YOU have held a reading glass at different distances from your eyes and have noticed that sometimes the images are large, at other times they are small, and often no image at all is visible. If you have never done this, do it now. Look through a reading glass at a small object and notice that its appearance changes as you move the glass back and forth.

To find out why this happens we have to determine how a lens controls light.

In the first place light travels very fast through air. It goes considerably slower through water, and even slower through glass. When light strikes a piece of glass or a container of water at an angle, the light is bent because its speed changes. This bending is called refraction. And refraction is what makes possible the control of light by a lens.

Here is an experiment that will show how the light is bent. Put a coin in a cup and back away or lower your head until the coin is just hidden by the edge of the cup. Without changing the position of your eyes, pour water into the cup carefully so the coin is not moved. If you cannot reach the cup comfortably have someone else pour in the water. When the water reaches a certain level, the coin will appear to rise from the bottom and become visible even though it really has not moved from its original position. Look at the illustration to see why this happened. When light from the coin struck the surface of the water at an angle, part of the light beam moved faster

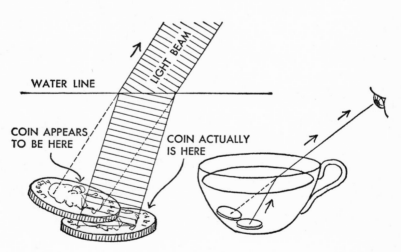

WATER LINE

LIGHT BEAM

COIN APPEARS
TO BE HERE

COIN ACTUALLY
IS HERE

than the other part, and this caused the beam to be bent. However, your eyes were not aware of this and they reported to the brain that the coin had been raised from the bottom.

It is as though the light beam leaving the water were a column of soldiers marching several abreast. Part of the file moved from a swampy area into a dry field, so it was speeded up. The rest of the column moved at its original speed and this caused the line of march to be "bent" or refracted.

Another way to see how this works is to place a large desk blotter or a piece of felt on a smooth table. (The blotter represents the water where speed is diminished; the table top represents the air where speed is increased.) Get two wheels and an axle from a toy train, car, or airplane, or make a set with Tinker Toy. Roll the wheels at an angle to the edge of the blotter so that one wheel hits the blotter before the other. Give them enough speed to go right over the rough area and out the other side onto the smooth table top again. The wheel tracks will be bent as the wheels enter the rough blotter because the wheel which hits the blotter first will be slowed down and will "hold the pivot," while the wheel on the table continues to travel rapidly. The tracks will be bent (turned) in the opposite direction as they leave the blotter.

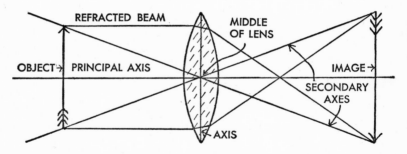

A similar thing happens when light enters a lens. As we look at a lens edge on, an imaginary line drawn from the top to the bottom is called an axis. A line at right angles to this and passing through the center of the lens is called the principal axis. Any light which strikes the lens along the principal axis goes right through without being bent. There is an infinite number of light rays, or beams, leaving every point of the object. We are interested in tracing only those beams which enable us to construct the image produced by the lens. The first of these beams is the one that goes directly through the center point of the lens (along the secondary axis in the diagram) and is not refracted. The second one is the refracted beam in the diagram.

We can learn a great deal about any lens or optical instrument if we accept three simple rules:

Rule 1: Any ray parallel to the principal axis will be bent so that it will be brought to a focus at a particular point on that axis.

Rule 2: Two of the rays of any light entering a lens will follow the secondary axes and will pass through the lens without being bent.

Rule 3: Whenever two rays of light meet after passing through a lens, a real (actual) image will be formed.

To see how your lens or reading glass brings light to a focus, hold the lens in a darkened room in a straight beam from a flashlight. Use a strong focusing flashlight and adjust it to the finest beam that you can get. Have someone blow smoke into the region around the light and the lens. Somewhere beyond the lens, about one foot with a reading glass, the light will be brought to a pinpoint. This is the focal point. The distance between this point and the axis of the lens is the focal distance.

Another way of determining the focal point and of measuring the focal distance of a lens is to hold it where it can focus a distant, brightly lighted scene on a piece of white paper. Note that the lens is collecting light from a

large area and bringing it to the screen. When you have arranged the lens and the paper to obtain the sharpest image possible, you have set the paper at the focal distance from the lens.

Now we are ready to find out how a single lens can produce so many varying images. The next few experiments should be done in a dark room, the darker the better. Support your lens in an upright position on a piece of newspaper or other large piece of paper that has been laid over a table top. Set the lens in modeling clay to hold it erect and then mark off the focal distance on both sides of the lens; also make marks at locations that are two times the focal distance.

Place a lighted candle 2 or 3 inches beyond twice the **focal distance as shown in the illustration here. Bring a**

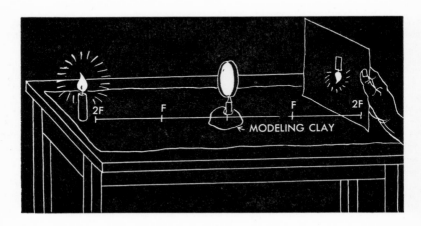

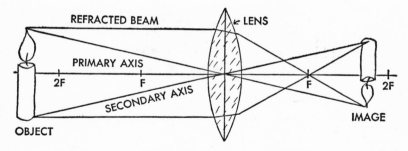

piece of paper between the two marks, *F* and *2F*, on the
other side of the lens and move it back and forth until a
sharp, inverted image smaller than the candle appears
on the paper. This is the way a lens is used in a camera.
If you let the paper represent the film, you can see how a
picture might be taken. When a lens is used in this way
the image is smaller than the object, and it is also inverted,
as are all real images.

Now move the lighted candle to the mark made at twice
the focal length as shown in the next illustration. The image that is formed on the paper will be the same size as

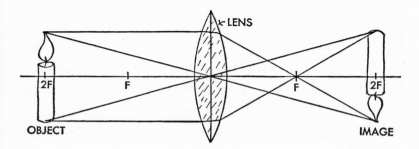

the candle, but it will be inverted. There are some life-size cameras that use this arrangement. Some telescopes use a lens like this in the eyepiece.

Place the lighted candle between the two marks on the paper, *F* and 2*F*, as shown. The image made on the upright piece of paper on the other side of the lens will be upside down as before, but this time the image will be considerably larger than the object—and it represents the

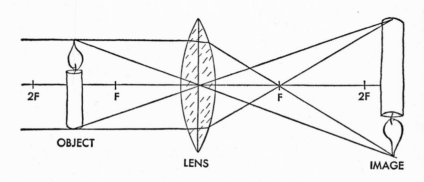

OBJECT **LENS** **IMAGE**

situation in a projector where a large image on a screen is desired. If you think of the candle as a lighted slide or a picture in a movie projector, perhaps you can see that the lens is serving as a device for projecting a larger image of the "slide" on a screen. Because the lens inverts the image, the slide must be upside down in the projector to make the image on the screen upright.

Now move the candle to the mark nearest the lens, the

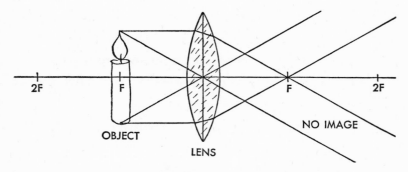

OBJECT

LENS

NO IMAGE

2F F F 2F

focal distance as shown here. When you hold the paper on the other side, no image forms at all because the light rays coming from the lens are parallel. Rule 3 indicated that rays had to meet on the image side of the lens if an image were to be formed. A lens with an object at the exact focal point produces no image at all.

The final possible position for the candle is between the lens and the focal point. Once again no image is seen when the screen is held up. The light coming through the lens

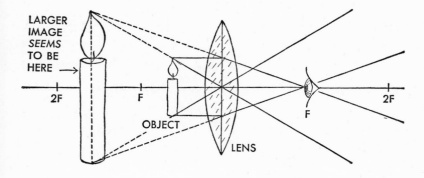

LARGER IMAGE SEEMS TO BE HERE →

2F F OBJECT LENS F 2F

is spreading out, therefore it never comes to a focus. However, if you look through the lens at the candle, you will see its image much larger—and right side up this time, as indicated by the dotted lines in the drawing. This is what happens when you use a lens as a reading glass. You want a larger, right-side-up image of the words in the book but you do not care to project them on a screen. The enlargement is caused by two conditions. First, light travels in straight lines up to a lens and then is bent according to the three rules. Second, we see an object, or its image in this case, in the last direction that light from it entered the eye. The light came from the candle in the directions indicated in the diagram. An extension of these directions (shown by the dotted lines) causes us to see an enlargement of the object.

A compound microscope is a specialized enlarger that uses two lenses, each with a different focal distance. As shown in the illustration here, the bottom lens is called the objective lens. The object, which is usually material mounted on a microscope slide and shown here with a small arrow, is placed just below the objective lens so that an enlarged, real image is formed near the viewing lens. The viewing lens, called the ocular, is located at the top of the microscope. If there were a screen inside the barrel of the microscope, an image would appear on it and the

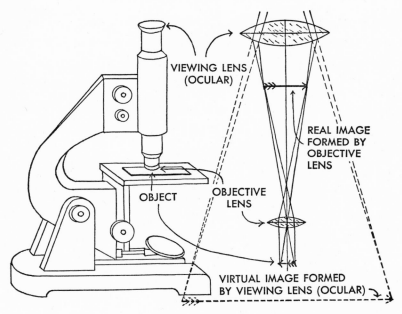

VIEWING LENS (OCULAR)

REAL IMAGE FORMED BY OBJECTIVE LENS

OBJECT

OBJECTIVE LENS

VIRTUAL IMAGE FORMED BY VIEWING LENS (OCULAR)

ocular would enlarge this inverted image a second time.

In a microscope the real image first formed is enlarged as many times as its distance from the objective lens is greater than the focal length of that lens. The distance is usually 150 millimeters, so if the objective lens has a focal length of 5 millimeters, the first image is 30 times greater than the object. If the ocular magnifies the image 10 times, the combination magnifies 10 times 30 or 300 diameters.

There is a type of telescope that also uses two lenses, but the arrangement is somewhat different. The image of the distant object is sharply formed at the focal point of

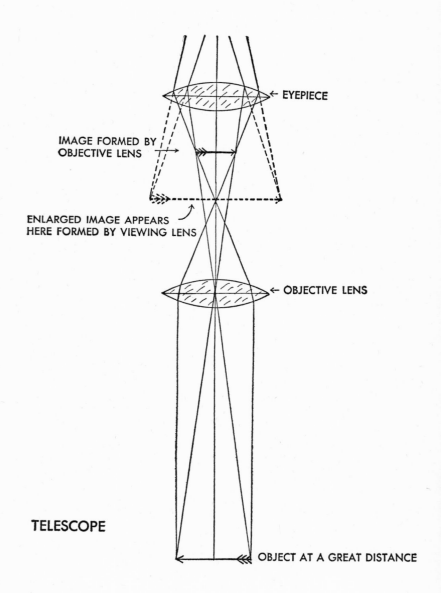

EYEPIECE

IMAGE FORMED BY
OBJECTIVE LENS

ENLARGED IMAGE APPEARS
HERE FORMED BY VIEWING LENS

OBJECTIVE LENS

TELESCOPE

OBJECT AT A GREAT DISTANCE

the first lens in the same way that you formed an image when determining the focal point of your reading glass. This image is then seen through a viewing glass and we see an enlargement of the object. A refracting telescope, which is the name given this type of instrument, may have a lens as large as 40 inches, which means it can gather a great deal of light and condense it into a bright image at the focal point. The eye then has the advantage of looking at this bright image much magnified by using the second lens.

Magnifying power is equal to the focal length of the objective divided by the focal length of the eyepiece. Therefore, to get a high magnifying power, the objective lens must have a long focal length. That is why telescope tubes are so long; an instrument with a 40-inch lens needs a tube 60 feet long—as tall as a 6-story building. This is the length of the tube of the Yerkes Observatory telescope in Williams Bay, Wisconsin.

There were many problems that had to be solved before optical instruments obtained the accuracy that they now have. But we are still a long way from perfection, and right now in many parts of the world scientists and engineers are at work trying to make better instruments so that a more perfect understanding of the world about us may result.

CHAPTER 8

EVERYDAY LENSES

TAKE A LOOK at an olive jar. Olives are most often sold in tall, narrow cylindrical jars. Packers do this not because the jars occupy less space on the grocer's shelf nor because the jars are easier to handle; they do it to make the olives appear to be larger than they are. The curved surface of the jar holds liquids in a sort of lens shape which makes jar and liquid act as a magnifier. You can prove it. Fill an olive jar with water and drop a marble in it. Measure the diameter of the marble before dropping it into the bottle and then measure it as accurately as you can by holding a ruler against the bottle when the marble is under water!

But we should not blame the olive packers for deceiving us, for many products are packed in this same manner. Many solid objects that are sold in round clear glass containers are enlarged in this way. Plums, cherries, prunes and peaches all look larger when you see them inside a clear glass jar. Try it and see for yourself.

Look through various clear glass containers, such as a quart jar, gallon jug, or soda bottle, at someone on the other side. See the different effects that are produced when the containers are empty and when they are filled with water.

A very simple way of seeing how effective a curved surface is as a magnifier is to put your finger in a glass of water and view it from the side. Your finger is normal size above the surface, but it is considerably enlarged beneath it. Look from the side at a pencil placed in water in a flat-sided bottle. The pencil is not magnified because you are viewing it through a flat surface.

Drops of water are also simple magnifiers. They are effective magnifiers, too. Place a single drop on a plate of glass and then look through the glass at an object. The curved surface of the drop serves the same function as did the curved surface of the jar.

You can make a somewhat more elaborate magnifier that uses the curved surface of water. Shape a piece of wire, about 3 inches long, around a nail to form as perfect a closed circle as possible. Dip the wire in water and a magnifier lens will be formed. The circle should be nearly perfect and the wire smooth, for best results. Experiment with different kinds of wire such as copper and iron, and use different size nails to see the various effects that are produced. You might try closing the circle by twisting the wire, or simply close it by putting the end of the wire against the shaft.

To determine how many times a magnifying glass enlarges an object, hold the lens in focus over a piece of ruled paper. Make a comparison between the number of *spaces* seen outside the lens and those seen inside it. If the ratio is 3 to 1, the lens is said to have a magnifying power of 3 diameters, or 3X. A water-drop lens may have a magnifying power of 2 to 3 diameters.

Read the advertisements for telescopes and microscopes carefully if you plan to buy one of the instruments. Some companies report the magnifying power of their products by multiplying the height magnification by the width magnification. They say that a 3-to-1 ratio lens magnifies things 9 times. Some companies tell the magnifying power of their lenses in diameters.

A very effective lens can be made from two watch glasses. These are pieces of glass shaped like small round dishes. (You may get these from a druggist or your science teacher, who uses them for evaporating dishes.) Invert one of the glasses over the other and, while holding them in this position, look through them. There will be no more noticeable difference than if you were looking with the unaided eye. This might be called an air lens, and, as you can see, it is not at all effective.

But we can change things by filling the space between the watch glasses with water. Do it in this manner. Slip a toothpick under one edge and put a piece of Scotch Tape across a diameter of one of the glasses and all the way around to the other side of the combination to hold them securely. Seal the joint between the two dishes, except where the toothpick enters and where the tape crosses, with clear adhesive such as the kind used for model airplane building. When this has set, remove the tape and fill the spaces that the tape has covered. Remove the toothpick and fill the lens with water by squeezing together one end of a soda straw, placing it in the crevice and then blowing water in. When the lens is full, seal it off with the

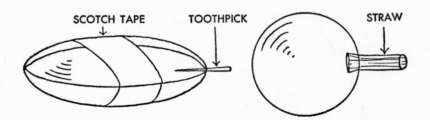

SCOTCH TAPE TOOTHPICK STRAW

same adhesive. After the adhesive has set, look through your lens and you will see that you have a good magnifier —the power depending upon the curvature of the glass itself.

This is called a double *convex* lens and you can see how it controls light by looking at the illustration here. Light coming from the object *AB* enters the lens obliquely and is therefore bent by it. The observer thinks that he sees the light coming from *CD* and so the object is magnified.

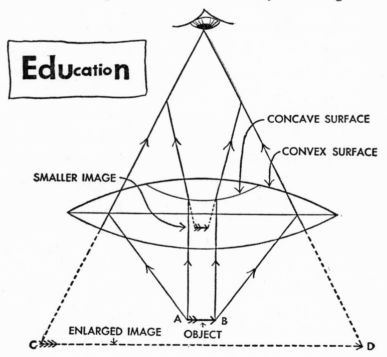

You can modify your lens and get an interesting combination of a *convex* lens and a *concave* one. Pierce the watertight layer around the lens in one spot and shake out some of the water until you have an air bubble inside it. Seal the hole and then hold the lens over a page of type and you will see magnified area surrounding a part of the page that has been made smaller. The part of the image that comes through the bubble (the surface of which is concave—sloped toward the center) appears smaller because the light rays entering the bubble are bent away from the bubble. They appear to be coming from small objects placed close to the bubble. The parts of the image coming through the water are magnified in the usual manner.

Look around you to see other lenses. Bent glass in church windows, fish bowls, and glass marbles are some you may have thought of already. Forest rangers warn against leaving bottles at camp sites. You can easily figure out why such bottles might become hazards; remember, they focus sunlight and so may cause fires.

CHAPTER 9

POLARIZED LIGHT

ORDINARY LIGHT can be made to perform some amazing tricks. But none of these tricks can match the capers of polarized light. Until a few years ago it would have been impossible for you to experiment with this type of light because the materials would have been too expensive. However, an inexpensive material has been made available that will help you experiment with this fascinating phase of light.

Light travels from place to place in waves. These waves are called *transverse* because they move back and forth at right angles to the direction the light is going. (The prefix *trans* means "across" in Latin.) Unlike waves in water, which appear to move up and down at the surface, light waves are believed to move in ripples in all directions in the space they are traveling through. It is difficult to visualize what scientists mean by light waves, but you can get some idea of how they operate by fastening a rope, a clothesline for example, to a doorknob and extending it 20 feet or so. Flip the rope up and down and a vertical wave will move along it. Or flip it sideways to produce a horizontal wave. Flipping it up and to the right or up and to the left will produce oblique waves also.

If the rope has a knot in it, you will observe the knot moving always at right angles to the direction of the wave. To make a model of a light beam you would need a multitude of ropes moving in all possible paths at the same instant in the space between you and the doorknob. This model would be impossible to build because the ropes would get in each other's way, but light, which is a form of energy and not a material, can manage it.

Under the proper conditions a beam of light can be produced in which only the waves which move in the same plane, say up and down, are moving in the beam. This kind of light can be made from ordinary light, if the horizontal and oblique waves are absorbed and only the vertical waves are allowed to move forward.

Remove one side of a large grocery carton made of corrugated paper. Cut a 1-inch slot in the side opposite the one you have taken out, as shown in the diagram. Put the free end of your rope through the slot and give it a flip toward the ceiling. The waves set up can pass along the rope unhampered because the slot is in the proper position to let the wave through. Now try flipping the rope to the left or right, parallel to the floor. The wave cannot get through the box now. It is stopped at the slot or is partly reflected back to your hand. That part of the rope extending from the far side of the slot is hardly affected. If you had several ropes threaded through the slot, and waves were moving in each one, the only wave to get through would be the one moving in a plane perpendicular to the floor. The slot would stop all the others.

Now set up a second box and slot similar to the first one. Arrange the boxes so that the slots are parallel. Pass the rope through both slots. Any wave which can get through the first box can get through the second one also. But now turn the second box on its side so that the slot in it is at right angles to the first one. A wave which can get through the first box is now stopped by the second.

The material which can sort out light waves as the cardboard boxes sorted out rope waves is called Polaroid. It is composed of many tiny crystals all standing side by side. The crystals are so tiny that the eye cannot detect them. They produce in effect a series of slots which comb

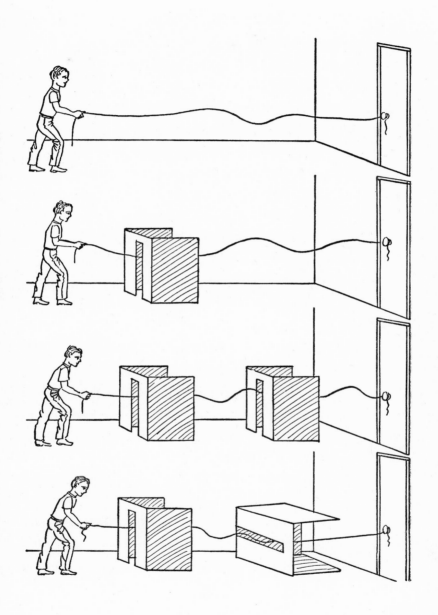

out the light vibrations. Only those which are all lined up in the same direction can get through. A beam of light which is composed of waves, or vibrations, all moving parallel to each other in this manner is called polarized light.

Pieces of Polaroid can be obtained occasionally from a theater which is showing a 3-D movie. A few years ago there were a number of 3-D movies shown in the theaters in the country and some theaters may still have a number of pairs of the kind of viewing glasses which were given to each patron. Much larger polarizing pieces may be obtained from a pair of discarded Polaroid sunglasses.

Get a pair of polarizing glasses and cut them apart at the bridge so that you have two separate eyepieces. Now place one piece over the other, face to face, so that they match exactly, and look through both toward a lighted lamp or other bright source of light. Note that a great deal of light gets through. Now hold one piece stationary and turn the other, still looking at the lighted lamp. Note that when the eyepieces are at right angles practically no light gets through.

The eyepiece nearest the light polarizes the light coming through it. When the crystals in the second filter are lined up with the crystals in the first, this polarized light comes right on through. It corresponds to the situation in the rope-and-box model where the parallel slots allowed a vertical wave to go through. When the invisible crystals are at right angles to each other, the first filter still produces a polarized beam, but it cannot get through the second filter and much of the light is shut out. This state of affairs corresponds to the crossed slots in the rope demonstration.

Polarizing filters have been suggested as an answer to the problem of night driving where the glare from oncoming headlights temporarily blinds the driver and makes every car moving toward him a potential hazard. Let a flashlight represent the headlight of an approaching automobile. Light the flashlight and place one eyepiece on it. Look at the light through the other polarizing piece. Note that, if you cross the pieces, the light coming from the flashlight is almost extinguished but that you can still see objects to the left and right of the light.

The suggestion for night driving is that all headlights be provided with polarizing glass with the invisible slots lined up in an oblique direction. The windshields of all automobiles would be made of similar glass or would have a section of the windshield so made and placed directly in front of the driver. This would mean that as you drove down the road at night, the headlights of any oncoming car would be sending out polarized light which would be exactly at right angles to the polarizing material in front of you in the windshield. Hence you could see the road and objects and people at the side of it illuminated by your headlights, but the oncoming headlights would only appear as a dull purplish blur. The scheme would not work, of course, unless all headlights and windshields were equipped, but the drop in the accident rate which would result makes the idea attractive enough to merit serious thought.

Most people are probably not aware of the fact that a great deal of the light we use to see by is polarized. As radiant energy from the sun strikes a reflecting surface, such as a sheet of glass, a polished table top, or a smooth road, much of the energy coming from the sun enters the shiny material and is absorbed; but those waves of radiant energy which are moving in one particular plane are reflected. These reflected waves are moving parallel to each other and so they make up a beam of polarized light. You know that in order to "skip" a stone from the surface of a river or pond, you must throw the stone so that it hits flat. If it lands edge first, it goes *kerplunk* and enters the water. It is somewhat the same with reflected light. The waves that hit "flat" are reflected in a beam of polarized light.

You can prove for yourself that much reflected light is polarized by observing a brightly lighted surface through one of your Polaroid films. Turn the piece slowly as you look through it and the glare or light directly reflected from the surface will disappear. In fact, you can look deep into a pond and see fish and water plants which are normally not visible because of the surface reflection. You can see signs on the road ahead of your car even though you are driving directly into the glare of a sunset. Polaroid sunglasses are popular with fishermen and other sportsmen because they can cut out glare this way. By placing the Polaroid films in eyeglass frames in such a way that the tiny crystals are at right angles to the polarized light coming from glaring surfaces, this troublesome reflected light is stopped before it gets to the eyes.

Now turn your single polarizing eyepiece on the sky. Do you discover that the sky is polarized too? It would seem reasonable to expect it to be, since the light from the sky is really reflected back from the atmosphere about us. If there were no atmosphere the sky would be completely black. Men who have gone aloft in high-altitude balloons have seen the stars out in the daytime because they get up to where the atmosphere is too thin to reflect sunlight back to their eyes.

Try looking at different portions of the blue sky. Are all portions equally polarized? Is the plane of polarization at the same angle for all parts of the sky? Place a piece of clear cellophane over the side of the eyepiece away from you so that the cellophane covers half of the opening. Turn the eyepiece through a complete circle and note that at one quarter of the turn the light from the sky (or any other source of polarized light) seen through the cellophane-Polaroid portion is brightest when the part seen through the Polaroid film alone is darkest. At another quarter the reverse is true. The cellophane nullifies the effect of the polarized molecules. You can easily tell when you get the maximum amount of darkening through the Polaroid film in this way because the contrast between the two halves is greatest then.

Note that clouds are not polarized. They are made of small droplets of water and each droplet reflects light in a different direction. A Polaroid filter placed in front of a camera lens can make wonderful cloud contrast pictures because it darkens the sky and does not affect the light from the clouds. The camera records bright clouds against a dark sky.

Turn your back to the sun and concentrate on the region of the sky exactly opposite the sun. Adjust the cellophane-Polaroid combination until one half is of maximum brightness—and the other half, naturally, maximum darkness. Hold the viewer at this angle and examine some other portions of the sky to the right and left of the first point. Note that the sky does not send back light from all portions of the sky at the same angle of polarization.

This little device you have made has been worked into a very practical direction finder for airmen and others who work in the polar regions above the 70th parallel of latitude. Imagine yourself an explorer lost in the wastes of the Arctic. Near the earth's pole the sun is below the horizon for long periods. This makes it impossible for you to determine location from the sun. Moreover, the twilight is so intense and lasts so long that the stars are not visible either. So you cannot use them to find where you are.

If you were in this spot you would think next of your magnetic compass and plan to find direction by that. But the earth's magnetic pole is up near where you are too, and an ordinary compass is affected by the presence of all sorts of stray magnetic fields. However, the polarized light from the sky can be detected easily—as you have just proved—and the direction of greatest polarization which is related to the position of the sun can be found readily at any time. If you had some means of determining your direction from the polarized light from the sky you could solve your problem neatly. Within very recent times such a device has been made and is in use in the polar regions by commercial and military fliers. Be sure to take one along the next time you go exploring in the Arctic!

Moonlight is light from the sun reflected from the surface of the moon. It is polarized, too, of course. Do you suppose that this may account for the odd effect which moonlight is reported to have on lovers? ("When I look at you in the moonlight, darling, I feel positively polarized!")

You can make a handy support for your Polaroid eyepieces by sliding them in between the teeth of an ordinary comb, as in the diagram. Arrange the films one behind the other in upright positions. They will then let through the least amount of light. Examine a piece of cellophane—or cellulose tape which has a cellophane base—as it is rotated between the two Polaroid pieces. You will observe a change of color beginning with red and continuing through other colors. When cellophane is made, the material is stretched as it is wound on rolls. This stretching lines up the molecules of which the film is made and makes them into a "light comb" of a slightly different sort than Polaroid film. The cellophane lets through two polarized beams at right angles to each other. One of these beams is slowed up more than the other in coming through the film. If white light enters the cellophane and a red wave gets through in a vertical beam, a green wave (com-

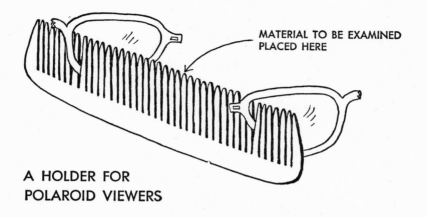

MATERIAL TO BE EXAMINED
PLACED HERE

A HOLDER FOR
POLAROID VIEWERS

plementary to red) may get through in a horizontal beam.
The eye cannot detect this fact. But a polarizing film will
let one of them through and block out the other.

As you rotate the cellophane, the Polaroid viewer will
first let one color through, and as you continue to turn the
viewer through a quarter-turn so that the left side becomes the top, you will see the complement of this color
coming through. Place several pieces of cellophane together in a pack and the effect is more pronounced since
each additional piece slows down the colored lights a little
more.

Make a cross of two pieces of Scotch Tape placed at
right angles. Examine this cross as you rotate it between
two Polaroid films. Note that the center of the cross, which
has two thicknesses of tape, allows blue light through

while the single thickness in the arms of the cross is transmitting yellow, the complement of blue. After it has been rotated through a quarter-turn, the arms appear blue and the square in the middle of the cross appears yellow. Making use of this property of cellophane you can make an extremely interesting gadget called a "step wedge," which will give you a range of colors beyond belief.

A step wedge is merely a collection of a varying number of pieces of cellophane. Cut 7 pieces of cellophane of the same width but make each one ½ inch shorter than the one before. Mount the longest one on a piece of window glass. A thin film of Vaseline will hold it on. Place the other pieces on the first one in order of decreasing length to make a set of cellophane "stairs," or "steps." Vaseline will hold these also. You will have a series of thicknesses of cellophane graded from 1 sheet to 7.

Examine the wedge between parallel Polaroid films and you will see that seven different colors appear. Each added sheet slows up the light just a little more and allows a different color to arrive at the polarizing screen in position to push its way through the parallel crystals. Cross the Polaroid films and you will find that each color will change to its complementary: the light blue becomes orange; the purple, light yellow; the red changes to green, and so on.

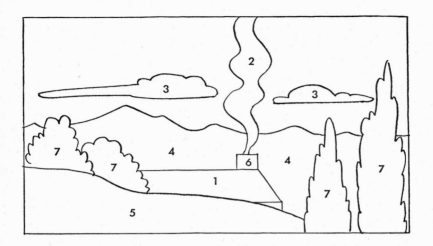

The colors seen through a polarizing film have a peculiar glowing quality not observable in any other natural object, and a picture made up of these colors is extremely interesting. The picture shown above is meant to be made from cellophane pieces and viewed through a polarizing screen. The figures on the picture indicate the number of thicknesses of cellophane needed for each particular part. In cutting the cellophane it is essential that all the pieces line up in the same direction that they lay in the original sheet. It is best to cut several pieces of cellophane from a sheet or roll and stack them up edge to edge. Stick the pieces together with Vaseline. Place the proper number of thicknesses over the part of the picture to be copied and cut out the part with a sharp razor. The section can then be transferred to the proper position on a glass plate and held on with Vaseline.

A picture as large as this cannot be viewed in its entirety with the two eyepieces you have. But, remembering that all reflected light is polarized, you can make a reflector which will spray the whole transparent picture from the back with polarized light. You may then observe it in full color through one of the small screens held to your eye. The diagram shows how to arrange this.

The reflector must not be lighted with a lamp directly. The light should first pass through a diffuser. The diffuser can be a piece of onionskin paper or other tissue. If you want to make a permanent diffuser, you may mount the

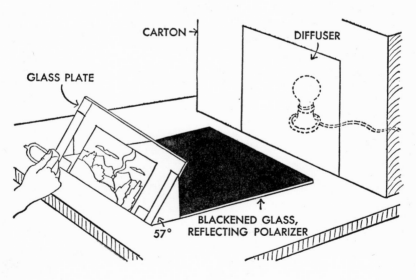

tissue between two plates of window glass. The reflecting polarizer is a piece of window glass painted with black enamel and placed paint side down on the table when dry. The picture appears best if it is supported at an angle of exactly 57 degrees from the table top and viewed through a Polaroid eyepiece held parallel to the picture.

Turn the Polaroid eyepiece in a circle until you have a clear sky. Then if the picture is made properly, you should have a light green foreground, red chimney, dark green trees, purple hills, and a very light yellow cloud. The roof will be brown. The smoke from the chimney, blue. Of course, as you rotate the Polaroid viewer you get a change in all these colors, so that at one time you may see pink trees and orange smoke. The picture provided here is only a suggestion. You may use your own imagination to create any number of fantastic effects.

Bending or twisting celluloid or other kinds of plastic puts a strain on it. The molecules in the bent or twisted part are stretched and twisted so that they line up differently from the way the molecules do in the other parts not under strain. Place a celluloid ruler, a plastic comb, or a transparent triangle from a drafting set between the crossed Polaroid pieces. Now twist or bend the plastic object. Note the appearance of bright streaks where the strain is greatest.

Engineers make plastic models of bridges or beams, place loads on them, and then examine them under polarized light to determine the places where the model is undergoing the most strain. Gear models may be examined while they operate. By this means designs may be improved before the actual device is built, a great deal of money may be saved, and new engineering knowledge may be obtained.

Glass from which telescope mirrors are to be made, such as the one in the 200-inch giant at Mt. Palomar, is examined in the same way to find whether the glass has any portions under strain due to fast cooling. Such strain patterns indicate a place where the glass would crack or warp during the grinding operation. The patterns might indicate that the mirror once made would not keep its true shape as it expanded and contracted with changes of temperature in the observatory.

These are only a few of the possibilities of this topic of polarization. It is obvious that the field for exploration in the subject is endless—and fascinating.

CHAPTER 10

PLANTS AND LIGHT

MANY ARTICLES in magazines and newspapers make us feel that atomic energy will bring a higher standard of living to the entire world, solve much of the food problem, and perform countless other wonders. It is suggested that the supply of energy that can be obtained from the nucleus of the atom is unlimited. This is not entirely true at present, for the supply of the few rare elements whose atoms can enter into nuclear reactions is definitely limited, and there is little promise that more of them will be found. The use of hydrogen in a fusion process may be the answer. But this idea needs a great deal of development.

But we do have a source of unlimited energy, as unlimited as anything in this world can be, and which has been with us since the beginning of the earth. And this source of energy is the sun.

A vast amount of energy falls upon the earth every hour of the day. To see how vast the amount is, use the focusing lens that you made in chapter eight, or use a reading glass. Take your lens outside on a clear, sunny day and focus sunlight to a small bright spot on a piece of newspaper. In a few moments, the paper will start burning because the radiant energy striking the whole area of the glass has been brought together to a small spot on the paper. Experiment with papers of different color to see if colors and textures affect the time required for them to start burning. Will brown paper ignite faster than newspaper? Black paper, which absorbs a great deal of the radiant energy which falls on it, should heat fastest of all. Does it? The area of the lens that you used is probably not greater than 16 square inches—yet the sunlight that fell upon that much area contained enough energy to set the paper on fire. Think of how much energy must fall upon a field, or upon an entire countryside.

For generations scientists have been trying to find a way of harnessing the sun and using the energy to drive engines directly; but so far they have not been entirely successful. There have been some partially successful efforts, but they have been on a small experimental scale.

Thus far nature has provided the best and cheapest device for converting the energy of the sun into a form that is useful to man. The green plant is a remarkable chemical factory that takes sun energy and uses it to convert water and carbon dioxide into carbohydrates that supply man and the other animals with the energy they need to survive. Much of the energy that is stored in plants is used by man directly when he consumes the plants as food. But large amounts of it are locked in wood, or in coal or oil or gas where it remains until we burn the fuel in furnaces or in engines. But even though the green plant is the best device that we have for trapping solar energy, it is a most inefficient one, for much of the energy that falls upon the plant is lost.

If green plants are dependent upon sunlight for their existence, then we should expect them to react to light in some way. The following experiments will show just how sensitive they are.

Plant some bean seeds in each of two glasses or coffee cans, and when the beans have grown their second leaves place one of the cans in a dark closet and leave the other one in sunlight. After two or three days you will see that the absence of light has a very noticeable effect on the sprouts in the closet, for they will be shorter than the other ones; they will be yellow in color and they will be more slender and weak.

Plants continually strive to seek light. In the tropical rain forests of South America plants crowd each other to get sunlight, often towering 120 feet and more to out-reach their competitors. You can see this in your own home.

Design a box similar to the one shown in the diagram. Cut up a cardboard carton and fasten together the pieces to make a carton 6 inches square and 18 inches high. Six inches from the bottom, fasten with gummed tape a 4-by-6-inch piece of cardboard to make a shelf. Six inches above this fasten a similar panel to make another shelf. Cut a 3-inch-square hole in the side of the box at the top. (You may wish to cut a small door at the bottom which can be opened to water the plant occasionally. If you do this, the door must be sealed light tight most of the time.) Put a vigorous plant inside the box (you may be able to use the bean plants that you raised for the experiment above) and place the carton so the window is toward the sunlight. The plant will strive so strongly to reach the light that it will grow around the cardboard shelves and eventually the tips of the vine will protrude from the opening at the top of the box. (Do not put the plant into the box until it is growing vigorously, for it needs a re-

94

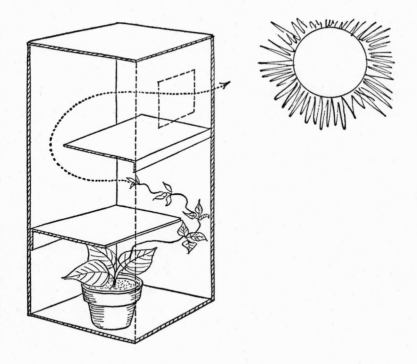

serve of strength to keep it going until it can reach the light.)

Light that comes from the sun seems to be all of a single kind, but it is made of waves of several kinds, some of which produce visible red, green, and blue light, and other waves which do not affect the eye at all but produce what is called infrared and ultraviolet. Not all of the parts of sunlight are important to plants. Botanists (those who study plants) have been experimenting for a long time to learn which part of the sunlight—the infrared or the ultraviolet, the red, green, or blue—is most useful to a plant. They have not reached a conclusion yet. Perhaps you would like to carry on an experiment to find out part of the answer for yourself. One way of doing this is as follows.

Plant some bean seeds in each of four coffee cans. Before planting the beans punch 6 holes around the can 1 inch from the top. Water them regularly. (You may prefer radishes because they develop more rapidly.) When the plants have attained a good growth, cover the coffee cans with cellophane, being careful to leave the holes open so that air can circulate around the plants. Cover one can with clear cellophane, another with red, the third one with green, and the fourth one with blue. Place all the cans in sunlight so that the only factor that is different in each one is the color of the cellophane cover. After the experiment has proceeded for a few days you should be in a position to determine which color of light has the most effect on the growth of your plants.

We cannot be sure what you will find, but on the basis of reasoning you might expect that the red light would have the best effect on plant growth. Objects appear green because they reflect that color. Green plants must therefore reflect a large part of the green light that falls upon them; and they must also absorb a large part of the red light. If they absorb red light, they probably need the light for growth. But then, they might absorb the blue light, and this might be the most important kind that they need. We cannot say. You will have to try the experiment to see what the answer is.

Men in laboratories work in just this manner. They figure out what they think might happen and then they develop an experiment, or perhaps a series of them, to check their judgment and to determine if what they think will happen actually takes place. "Let's try it and see" is a phrase heard frequently in a laboratory. Make it part of your thinking and you will be in a better position to get true answers.

CHAPTER 11

VIEWING SNAPSHOTS IN 3-D

IF YOU HAVE seen 3-D movies, you know how the illusion of depth adds greatly to the appearance of the pictures. How would you like to add the third dimension to your old snapshots and see your friends as they really were? Actually 3-D movies are made with two cameras placed at a small distance apart and obviously it is too late to go back and take all your old snapshots over again. But a handbag mirror and a lens can be set up to give a startling appearance of depth to any photo.

The best lens to use is one with a long focus, a lens which gives sharp images of objects placed 10 to 20 inches away. Some eyeglass lenses are fine but an ordinary hand magnifying glass will work fairly well. Place the snapshot on the table with the bottom of the picture facing away from you under a brightly lighted lamp with a dark shade. Examine the picture with the lens and find the distance at which the picture appears most sharp. Take note of this distance. Now hold a rectangular handbag mirror over the table at about this distance from the picture. Tip the mirror so you can see part of the picture reflected in it. Look at the reflection with the lens. The mirror and lens should be in shadow. With a little adjustment of distances and the angle of the mirror the snapshot will take on an appearance of depth. Objects in the foreground will stand out sharply from the background. The illusion is best in pictures with good contrast, those having very dark parts and very light parts.

If you want to make a convenient viewing box and do away with the need for adjusting the mirror each time, get a shoe box and paint the inside with dull black paint or with India ink. Cut an opening about 3 inches wide and across the whole width of the bottom of the box near one end. This is to be used as a place to insert the pictures.

Find the best viewing distance for the lens you have. This will be the distance at which the image is sharpest. Now fit the mirror into the box at such a place that the distance from the picture to the center of the mirror, plus the distance from the mirror to the top of the box, will be equal to the best viewing distance. Since the mirror will

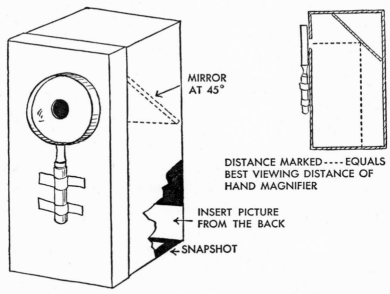

MIRROR
AT 45°

DISTANCE MARKED ---- EQUALS
BEST VIEWING DISTANCE OF
HAND MAGNIFIER

INSERT PICTURE
FROM THE BACK

SNAPSHOT

A 3-D SNAPSHOT VIEWER

probably be too small to fit the box, you will need to make
a cardboard frame to just fit the box. Tape the mirror to
the frame. The mirror frame should be placed in the box
at an angle of exactly 45 degrees. Fold a piece of paper so
that the right side edge lies along the top edge and use
this as a guide. Secure the mirror and its frame in the shoe
box with paper tape. Place the cover on the box and cut a
hole about the size of a nickel in the cover at a point across
from the center of the mirror. Fasten the lens over this
hole with paper tape. If the lens is of the long focus va-

riety, the viewing hole will be near the top of the box, but with most hand lenses the hole will be much nearer the bottom.

Now slip in a snapshot with the top of the picture placed closest to you, place the viewer where sunlight or other bright light can strike the picture and see your old friends in modern 3-D.

The illusion is partly due to the double image produced by the mirror. If you look closely through the lens at parts of the picture in the mirror, you will see that there is a sharp image formed by the reflection from the silvered back of the mirror and another fainter one quite near the first which has been formed by reflection from the glass surface of the mirror. Sometimes this second fainter image gives things in the foreground of the picture the appearance of being cut out of cardboard and placed against the background of the picture.

Don't do without Technicolor in your viewer! Colored photographs from magazines show up in 3-D too. The only drawback to the colored pictures is that the magnifying process brings out the little colored dots which are used to print the pictures. If you have never looked at a colored picture through a magnifying glass this in itself may startle you and give you a new lead for experiments with light.

CHAPTER 12

A WATER-DROP MICROSCOPE

IT WOULD be difficult to make a listing of the benefits that have resulted from the invention of the microscope, for discoveries are being made continually. Even while you are reading this book, hundreds of researchers are peering into microscopes looking for more complete answers to the causes of disease, the structure of matter, and countless other problems.

Modern microscopes using glass lenses are expensive and complicated instruments which can produce magnifications up to 2,000 times. A baseball bat magnified this many times would appear a mile long. The electron microscope which is even more expensive and complicated, produces the greatest magnifications (10,000 to 12,000 times), and pictures taken with it may be enlarged so that magnifications of 100,000 times result. The baseball bat would be 50 miles long on this scale.

Anton van Leeuwenhoek, a Dutchman who lived in the sixteenth century, and the first man to report that he had seen bacteria, did most of his work with simple microscopes consisting of a single tiny lens. You can follow his idea and make a microscope which uses a single drop of water for a lens, like the water-drop lens in chapter eight, and achieve some surprising results.

But to start off, experiment with the simplest magnifier, a postcard with a pinhole in it. Put a pinhole in the middle of the space at the right of the card usually reserved for the address. Hold the card as close to your face as possible and look through the hole at a pin held in your other hand. Because the pinhole allows so little light to come through, you will get the best results by holding the pin under a lamp so that it is brightly illuminated. Bring the pin up to the hole slowly, keeping it in view, and you will find that it appears larger and larger as it approaches. When it is almost touching the card, it appears enormous. Do the same with the edge of a leaf, a flower petal, or a pencil point. If you examine your finger this way, the ridges of the tip will look like small hills.

The pinhole makes it possible for you to bring objects closer to your eye and still keep them in focus; therefore

103

you are able to examine them at a much closer distance than you do ordinarily. That is why they look so large. They also look dim unless they are very brightly lighted because the pinhole allows only a very little light to go through.

To show how the amount of light that enters the eye is cut down, look through the pinhole at the top of a lighted 60-watt lamp. Ordinarily the lamp is so bright when lighted that it is difficult, if not impossible, when looking straight at it, to read the printing on the lamp which indicates the company that made it and its rating in watts. Through the pinhole the reading is clear, and no discomfort is felt when you look directly at the lighted lamp.

Now let us construct a real microscope, something that actually enlarges objects, using a lens. You will need a piece of postcard, a piece of metal foil from a candy bar or cheese package, a needle, and a drop of water. Cut the piece of postcard into an egg shape just large enough to fit into your eye like a monocle. Punch or cut a ½-inch hole in the center of the card.

Cut a piece of foil a little smaller than the piece of postcard, smooth it out carefully and glue it to the card so it covers the hole. Hold the foil against another piece of cardboard, or a blotter, and punch a perfectly round hole in the foil with a needle. Now use a toothpick to spread a thin layer of Vaseline around the hole on each side of the foil.

With the small end of another toothpick place one small drop of water in the hole in the foil. To keep the drop from being blotted up on the bottom side, support the cardboard over the inverted top of the Vaseline jar while you are adding the water. Use care so that the drop fills the hole exactly and bumps up on either side of the foil. The droplet is now a lens capable of magnifying as much as a hundred times or more.

To use the microscope, place the monocle containing the droplet lens in your eye and face a lighted 60-watt lamp. Bring the tip of a pencil close to the drop and hold it as still as possible. It will be necessary to move the pencil about ever so slightly until you get the best magnification. The pencil point will look tremendous. Look at other objects. The veins in the wing of a fly will look like a series of railroad tracks, and a human hair will look like a large pipe. Leeuwenhoek arranged a needle attached to a threaded screw and fixed to a board so that he could place his objects before the water-drop lens easily.

If the lamp is too bright, the background will appear to be a glare. Place a piece of paper with a round hole in it between your monocle and the light to cut down the amount of light hitting the object. Then cover the other eye. Experiment with various size holes in the paper and work at varying distances from the lamp until you find the right conditions. In using this microscope, as in the more complicated ones, light conditions are extremely important.

The lens will evaporate eventually, or you will touch it with an object that you have brought too close to it, or you will wink it off; but you will soon become expert at replacing the water-droplet lens. A small amount of glycerin from the drugstore will make a better lens, since it does not evaporate, and a droplet of it will produce larger images because glycerin bends light more than water does.

Any effort you make to improve your ability to form lenses or to mount the objects you examine will repay you amply, and the water-drop microscope will provide you with hours of amusement and with much new knowledge. If you can borrow prepared microscope slides from your science teacher, you will find that your simple microscope will enlarge them very well.

CHAPTER 13

A "MAGIC" BOX

A PIECE of ordinary window glass can either reflect light
or let it go through, depending upon how light falls upon
it. Hold a flashlight behind a piece of window glass and
shine the light toward you. When the glass and light are
arranged in this manner, the glass acts as a good trans-
mitter for the light. All but a small amount of energy from
the flashlight gets through the glass.

But the glass can be made into a reflector by setting it
up as shown in the illustration on p. 108. The glass will
stay upright if it is set in a lump of clay or if it is supported
by spring-type clothespins. Make sure the glass is clean
and then place a lighted candle in front of the glass. An
image of the candle will be apparent. Incidentally, this
image will appear as far in back of the pane of glass as the

candle itself is in front of it. In fact, you can measure the distance that the candle is in front of the pane, and then place a glass of water the same distance in back of the pane; and the candle will appear to be burning in a glass of water.

You can make use of the fact that glass either reflects or transmits light, depending upon the lighting, by making a "magic" box—a device that can be used to make a very interesting and bewildering effect.

You can modify the dimensions given in the following explanation to fit the wood and glass that you have to work with. Make a wooden box about 18 inches square and 12 inches high and partition it part way along the diagonal with a board 12 by 16½ inches. Nail a board that measures 9 by 12 inches at right angles to this partition. We can call this our "baffle board." Fasten narrow supporting strips to this baffle board and to the adjacent corner and slide between these a 9-by-12-inch piece of clean window glass. Over half of the diagonal partition is wood and the remainder is glass. Fasten lamp fixtures (miniature sockets) behind the baffle board as shown in the illustration. Hook the wires together as shown and attach them to the 14-volt take-off on a train transformer.

If you do not have miniature lamp sockets you can make them very easily with a piece of wood about 2 inches square for the base. Bend a piece of wire about 3 inches long around a pencil to spiral it and then fasten the wire to the block of wood as shown. Fasten the other lead-in wire to another screw placed so that the base of the bulb rests upon it.

Put switches in the wires so that either one set of bulbs may be turned on alone, or so that they may both be turned on at the same time.

Switches may be made from two strips of tin from a tin can each ½ inch wide and 2½ inches long. Make right-angle bends ½ inch from each end of one piece of the tin and fasten it to the edge of a block of wood 2 by 3 inches

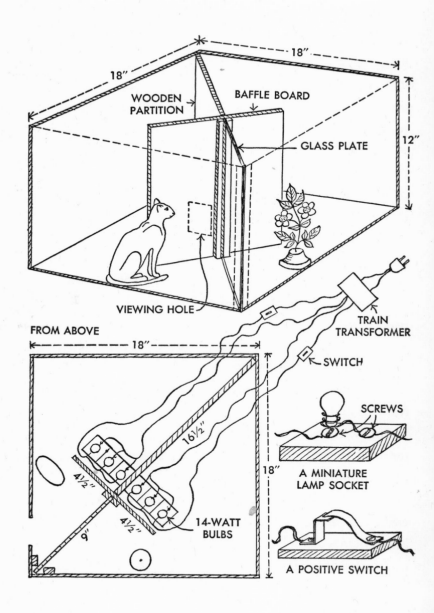

18"

18"

WOODEN
PARTITION

BAFFLE BOARD

12"

GLASS PLATE

VIEWING HOLE

TRAIN
TRANSFORMER

FROM ABOVE

18"

SWITCH

16½"

SCREWS

4½"

18"

A MINIATURE
LAMP SOCKET

4½"

9"

14-WATT
BULBS

A POSITIVE SWITCH

as shown in the illustration. The other piece is screwed down and then bent so that it can be pushed against the upright piece to make contact. If you wish to leave the switch closed, simply hook the diagonal piece under the lip of the upright section.

Cut a viewing hole in the side of the box as indicated in the drawing. The opening should be about 2 inches square and the top of it should be about 4 inches from the top of the box. Blacken the inside of the box completely by coating it with a flat black paint or by pasting black paper over the surface. Polish the plate of glass so that there are no dust specks on it.

Place objects in the locations noted in the figure. We used a small statue and a spray of flowers. You may use anything at all so long as they fit into the space easily. Cover the box and you are ready to go.

Sight through the hole and turn on one of the sets of lights. Let us say you started by turning on the right hand lights, then the flowers will become visible. Turn out these lights and you can make the statue become visible by reflection apparently in the same place by lighting the other set of bulbs. Try lighting only one bulb on one side while all the bulbs are lit on the other side to see what kind of effect is produced.

Try the "magic" box on your friends. Perhaps they will

be fooled completely; but, on the other hand, they may come up with a plan for improving on this design.

Magicians use a box somewhat like this one for a "talking head" trick.

A square table the size of a card table is placed near one end of a room. Heavy black material covers the top and the ends. The space in front is not covered. Two mirrors are placed at right angles under the table in the center section. An observer sees the front legs of the table and their reflections in the mirrors. Because he can see four legs, he believes the space under the table is empty.

The magician's assistant gets behind the mirrors and puts his head through a hole in the table top. Dim green lights play upon the head so that the audience thinks it is seeing a human head removed from the body. It is a very weird effect. When the head begins to talk and move, people in the audience are given quite a start.

Sometimes in stage shows "ghosts" are made to move right through the body of a living actor. Here again the magic box idea is applied. There are two stage levels as shown in the drawing. The audience looks directly through the upper glass in the drawing and sees the living actors. An actor playing the "ghost" moves on the lower stage and his image is reflected from the lower mirror to the upper glass and then from there to the audi ence. The audience sees the actors and the ghost at the same time and so the ghost may appear to move right through people, chairs, or other objects placed on the upper level.

Light can be made to do strange things; but in every case basic principles remain unchanged.

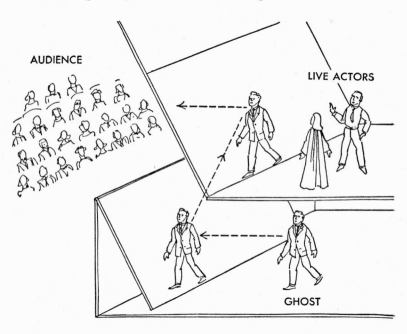

CHAPTER 14

THE KALEIDOSCOPE

THE KALEIDOSCOPE, a device for producing intricate patterns from a few bits of broken glass, has fascinated people for over a hundred years. Since nearly everyone is familiar with the toy, let's make one so we can find out how it works. Two pieces of window glass of about equal size are set up on books as shown in the diagram. The bottom piece of glass is held in place by inserting it between the leaves of one of the books near the top of the pile about 1 inch from the top covers. A piece of tissue paper or onionskin paper placed on top of this piece of glass and held by the book leaves will serve as a diffusing screen.

Take a small electric lamp and pile up books until the stack is high enough to make it possible to place the bottom glass plate an inch or so above the bulb of the lamp. Use a 60-watt bulb.

Get two rectangular mirrors of nearly the same size, or have your hardware man cut two equal-sized pieces from an old mirror. Using one of the pieces of mirror as a pattern, cut a piece of cardboard the exact size of the mirror. Stand the mirrors and the cardboard on their shorter edges in the form of a triangle with the mirror sides toward the inside. Snap two rubber bands around them to hold them together and place them on the top piece of window glass. Cut or tear pieces of colored cellophane into small bits about the size of the eraser on a pencil. Colored bits of paper can be used but transparent cellophane is best. The more irregular the pieces, the better. Place these on the bottom glass just beneath the upright mirrors and place the lamp so that the pieces are brightly lighted from below. Look down through the opening between the mirrors and adjust the mirrors if necessary until a design appears. Moving the colored bits on the paper with a stick will produce another design, and the number of designs you can make is practically without limit.

Now let's see *why* it works. Place the corner of the triangular base which is made by the upright mirrors over a single piece of cellophane or paper. Note the image that you see when you look down into the device. The piece

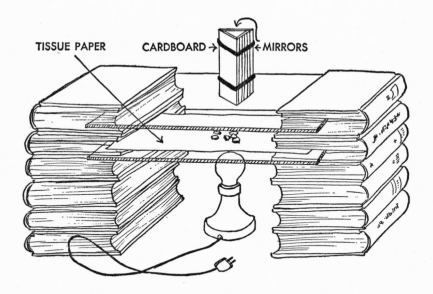

TISSUE PAPER   **CARDBOARD →**   **← MIRRORS**

appears to be multiplied by 6; in other words, you can see the original piece and 5 images of it. *All* colored pieces which fall inside the triangle formed by the mirrors will appear sixfold. Therefore the designs you see are all like 6-petaled flowers or 6-pointed snowflakes.

Since the mirrors and the cardboard are all the same size, they form an equal-angled triangle; therefore, each angle between the pieces is 60 degrees. This produces sixfold images. Now remove the cardboard and change the opening between the mirrors to 30 degrees. Measure the angle with a protractor. Now the multiplication of images is twelvefold; but images occur in pairs so that we

116

still see a 6-pointed flower or star arrangement, but the design is more intricate.

With the cardboard removed from the third side of the triangle, place a crumpled piece of colored cloth between the mirrors. Light the cloth from the side. The multiplication that takes place in the mirrors turns the cloth into a beautiful 6-petaled flower which appears in 3 dimensions. A white handkerchief will produce lovely white flowers, while colored silks produce some breathtaking effects.

A more permanent kaleidoscope can be made quite easily and you can produce designs whenever you wish. You will need a mailing tube or the cardboard core from a roll of kitchen paper towels. Get an old mirror or buy a cheap one from which you can cut pieces with a glass cutter. If it is impossible to get mirror pieces, you can cut single-thickness window glass and paint one face of each of the pieces with black enamel. It is also possible to use two pieces of shiny aluminum.

A great deal depends upon getting the proper width for the mirror pieces. To do this, place the end of the mailing tube on a piece of paper and draw carefully around it. Now with a compass draw a second circle just inside the first and as nearly the diameter of the inside of the tube as you can estimate. From any point of the inner circle lay out a 60-degree angle. Use a protractor for this, with the base of the protractor forming a tangent to the circle and measure the angle very carefully. Extend the sides of the 60-degree angle until they touch the circle. These lines will be the width of mirror you will need in order to fit the tube exactly. The length of the pieces of mirror can be 3 inches or more.

Fasten the two pieces of mirror together lengthwise with cellulose tape or masking tape. Cut the tube the same length as the mirrors. Glue the mirrors to the inside of the cardboard tube by covering the edges of the mirror glass with a thick layer of quick-drying glue or cement and then sliding them into the tube.

Cut a strip of cardboard 2 inches wide and just long enough to fit snugly around the mailing tube. Fasten the strip together and slip the ring so made over the end of the mailing tube. Be sure that it fits snugly but that it can still be turned. Now get some clear heavy plastic. Transparent plastic boxes and cigarette package holders are available which will do nicely. With a fine-tooth saw, cut out a disk of plastic that will just fit inside the 2-inch cardboard cylinder. You will have the right size piece if you stand the mailing tube upright on the plastic and draw around it with a crayon. Cut the plastic just inside the crayon mark.

Make a similar disk from frosted or translucent plastic.

A clear piece of plastic may be made translucent by rubbing it with fine emery paper wet with water.

If you cannot locate the proper sort of plastic, the disks can be cut from glass. First draw the proper size circle on a small piece of single-thickness window glass or the glass used in mounting pictures. Fill a large dishpan with water and hold the piece of glass under the water. Take a pair of tin snips or heavy scissors in the other hand and, holding both the tin snips and the glass under water, cut the glass to a disk shape. Cut a very little at a time, opening the jaws of the snips as wide as possible and cutting close to the pivot. Cut just slightly within the crayon marks. The edge of the glass will be jagged, like saw teeth, and should be handled with care. The disks when cut should, of course, just fit inside the 2-inch-high cardboard cylinder. One glass disk must be frosted. You can do this by rubbing it on another piece of glass on which a little valve-grinding compound has been placed. You can get the compound at a neighborhood garage or auto supply store.

Cut out 3 strips of cardboard, each ¼-inch wide and long enough to go around the *inside* of the 2-inch-high cylinder. Glue one of the strips inside the cylinder so that it is flush with the edge. Place the frosted plastic or glass disk inside the tube so it rests on this cardboard flange. If you wish, a bit of fast-drying glue can be run along the edge of the glass to help hold it securely.

Now get some colored glass and break it into pieces about ¼ inch across. You can obtain colored glass from marbles, bottles, and jars. Break the glass by placing it in heavy paper or cloth bags and striking it with a hammer. Paste another strip of cardboard inside the cylinder and against the frosted disk to hold it in position. Drop a few bits of colored glass on top of the disk, enough to cover about ¼ of it. The bits of glass should be of such a size that they can change position between the two disks but not so small that they fall to the bottom in a heap. Now place the clear glass disk in the cylinder so that it rests on the second cardboard flange, and hold it there by gluing the third narrow strip around the inside of the cylinder and snug against it. Slide the small-diameter cylinder containing the mirrors into the end of the large-diameter cylinder holding the bits of glass. The large-diameter cylinder should fit well enough to keep it from falling off but should be loose enough to turn with ease.

The next job is to make an eyepiece. Cover the end of the long tube with gummed paper. Find the center of the end and mark a circle large enough to just touch each of the mirrors. Carefully cut this out with the corner of a razor blade. Point your kaleidoscope at a light, look

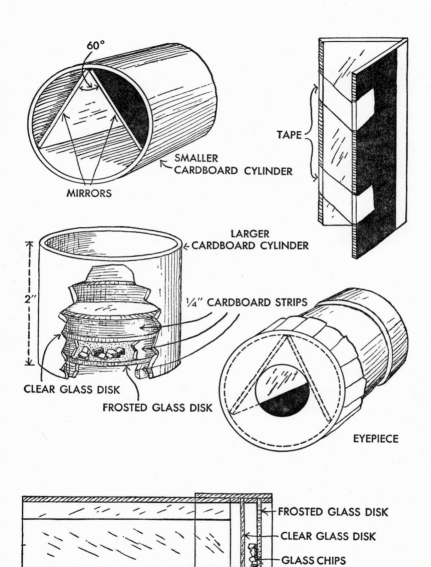

60°

MIRRORS

SMALLER
CARDBOARD CYLINDER

TAPE

LARGER
CARDBOARD CYLINDER

2"

¼" CARDBOARD STRIPS

CLEAR GLASS DISK

FROSTED GLASS DISK

EYEPIECE

FROSTED GLASS DISK

CLEAR GLASS DISK

GLASS CHIPS

through the eyepiece, and you will see a beautiful 6-pointed design. Shake the tube and the design will change, or turn the large-diameter tube while looking through the eyepiece and you will see a series of designs, one following the other and each one different from the last. There is no end to the variety of the formations that you can make. It's all done with mirrors, for you are seeing multiple images of the pile of glass particles between the two glass disks.

If the design is not uniform and radiating evenly from a central spot, it is probably because the mirrors are not at an exact 60-degree angle. Take them out of their tube and measure the angle carefully. Adjust if necessary and re-insert them.

If you wish to project the beautiful patterns from your kaleidoscope, you will have to build one with three mirrors of exactly the same width. Construct the instrument as has been described here, laying out a 60-degree angle when determining the size of mirror pieces to be used.

Get a large cardboard carton and make a hole in one end exactly the size of the larger end of the kaleidoscope. Place a 100-watt lamp in the cardboard box and hold the larger end of the kaleidoscope up to the hole. For a more permanent job, the instrument may be held in the hole with paper tape. Now hold a hand magnifying glass near the eyepiece in the position normally occupied by the eye when viewing the image. The lens will project a real image on a sheet of white paper placed about 3 feet away. You may have to adjust the white paper screen until the sharpest image is obtained. Designs may be projected this way so they may be enjoyed by several people at once or so they may be copied and preserved.

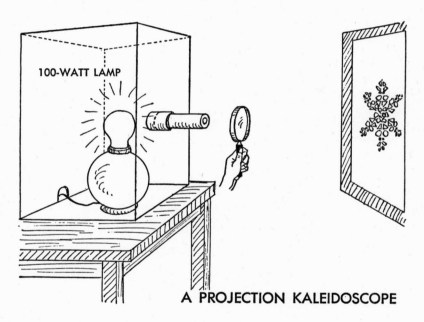

100-WATT LAMP

A PROJECTION KALEIDOSCOPE

CHAPTER 15

THE STROBOSCOPE

HAVE YOU ever noticed that when automobiles start up in the movies the wheels at first appear to go backward? This is particularly true in old movies made when cars had wheels with spokes.

Have you ever watched an electric fan start up when it was lighted by an electric lamp? There is a time when the motion of the fan seems to be backward. The wheels of real automobiles don't go backward when the car is moving ahead, and a fan in daylight starts up without any apparent backward motion.

The problem of automobile wheels in the moving pictures is easily explained. The projector is actually showing a series of still pictures with darkness in between. Each picture shows the whole car a little farther along its path but the wheels may not have turned over through a complete turn. Therefore a spot at the top of the wheel in the first picture may not have turned around to a place ahead of itself on the wheel when the next picture was taken. If it has arrived at a place behind the first position, the spot on the wheel appears to be moving in a direction opposite to the direction which the wheel is turning.

The problem of the backward-moving fan is answered in somewhat the same way. The difference lies in the source of light itself. An electric lamp which runs on alternating current is supplied with current for a short interval and then the current stops. Another burst of electricity then moves through the lamp in the other direction. The lamp is lighted brightly only while current flows in it. Actually the filament is never completely cool so that there is not a sharp difference between dark and light.

A fluorescent lamp produces a much sharper difference between light and no light. If you are reading under a single fluorescent tube lamp, you are spending half your time in the dark. The light turns on and off 60 times a second. This is so fast that the eye cannot detect the alternate periods of dark and light.

If the blades of a fan were to turn around exactly 60 times each second so that one blade always arrived in the upright position just as the light from the fluorescent lamp turned on, this blade would be lighted just as it got into the upright position. But it would move around most of its way in the dark. It would come back to the upright position just as the light flashed again. You would see the blade only when it was lighted, of course. (You can't see things in the dark, you know.) The fan, therefore, would appear to stand still. This effect is called the stroboscope effect and is of great value to engineers and scientists who work with fast rotating objects.

You can experiment with this stroboscopic effect with some easily obtained materials. Cut out a 4-inch circle from a piece of white cardboard and divide the circle into 4 equal sectors by drawing 2 diameters at right angles to each other. Now divide each of the sectors in two. You will then have 8 sections shaped like pieces of pie. Paint every other one with black tempera paint or India ink.

Now mount the cardboard circle on a hand drill by pushing a stout, short nail down through the center of the circle and grasping it in the chuck of the drill. Hold the drill as the girl is doing in the diagram, under a bright lamp bulb or fluorescent light.

Turn the handle of the drill and observe the black and white sectors carefully. With a little practice you can turn the drill at just the right speed to have the sectors appear

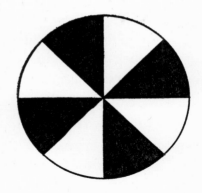

to be at rest. If you go slower than this speed, the sectors will seem to go backward. Increase your speed and the sectors will move ahead.

Actually you need to have the circle turning only 15 revolutions a second to stop the motion. The black sections (or the white) follow each other during each quarter of a circle. During the $\frac{1}{120}$ second that the light is out, the next white section of the circle must move around and take the place of the first white section.

If you look at the gears on your drill, you will see that every time you turn the handle around once the wheel revolves several times so that you don't have to turn the drill handle at a very fast rate to have the circle move around 15 times a second. Try it.

The stroboscope is used by engineers to examine flywheels while they are in motion. The stroboscope is a light which flashes on and off at a certain rate and produces a bright light followed by complete darkness. Sometimes a crack develops in a wheel but the crack only opens up while the wheel is in motion. When the machine stops, the crack closes and cannot be located. By using a stroboscope which goes on and off at the proper time, the wheel can be made to appear at rest and it can then be examined for the flaw.

Automobile repairmen use the stroboscope to find out if the crankshaft of a car is turning over at the proper speed for efficient operation of the car. There are many more uses for this handy device.

CHAPTER 16

HALOES AND CORONAS

LIGHT IS bent when it moves between lines ruled close together on glass. Somewhat the same thing happens when
light moves through a glass plate which is covered with a
thin layer of dust. The dust particles keep out light; but
the spaces between the particles bend any light that goes
through the glass. Since the particles are scattered in all
directions on the glass plate, the collection of spaces between them bends the light out in all directions.

The result is a circle of light. Everyone has seen such a
circle in the "ring around the moon." Sometimes we see a
ring around the sun also. If you have been very careful in
your observations, you have noticed that these rings come
in two varieties. One kind has a radius of about 22 degrees
and the other a radius of 46 degrees. These angles are exactly the ones which result when sunlight is bent by

6-sided ice crystals. For this reason it is thought that these rings appear only when a certain type of ice crystals is present in the high, cirrus clouds. A ring made by light passing through ice crystals is called a halo.

When the clouds are lower and composed of tiny water droplets the ring may be either white or made of all the separate colors of the spectrum. This kind of ring is called a corona.

You can show this corona effect by breathing on a cooled piece of glass plate and looking through it at a distant light. Thoroughly clean a plate of glass and leave it in the refrigerator for an hour or so. Then blow over it a couple of times to fog up the glass. The spaces between the tiny droplets of moisture serve to bend the light and a colored circle shows up around the brightly illuminated central spot. If in addition you lightly dust talcum powder on it, the effect is heightened and can be observed for a longer time, since the talcum particles do not evaporate as water droplets do.

The delicate colors of the corona are frequently lost in this method of observation because of the intense brightness of the central spot which partly blinds our eyes to what is appearing in the rim next to the spot. A better method for observing the corona is to set up a cardboard carton with a hole in one end large enough to admit an ordinary electric light socket. Exactly opposite it across the carton push in a pencil point to make a hole about ⅛ inch across. From this hole a thin beam of light will issue.

About a foot away from this carton set up a second one, the end of which has been covered with white paper. With a hand reading glass focus the thin beam of light on the white paper. Draw a line just outside the circle formed by the light and cut this out with a sharp knife. Now when the beam is brought to a focus the bright spot will disappear into the box. It helps if the box is lined with dark paper so that all light from the central beam is lost.

Darken the room completely and focus the beam into the hole. Now hold the glass plate that is covered with moisture or talcum powder between the lens and the white paper screen. A corona will appear which will show

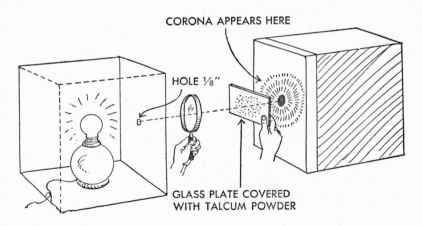

CORONA APPEARS HERE

HOLE ⅛"

GLASS PLATE COVERED WITH TALCUM POWDER

a spectrum of the most delicate tints. It is quite startling to see how the placing of the powder-covered plate in the beam lights up the whole screen with an eerie light. When a "ring around the moon" occurs, you can see this peculiar light shining on objects all around.

This same scattering of light by small particles is the cause of the colors of the sunset. You may have noticed that the most brilliant sunsets come at the close of hot, dry days. The particles of dust which have risen break up white light into its colors. After Krakatao, a volcano in the South Pacific, erupted violently at the beginning of the century, the dust completely circled the globe and produced spectacular sunsets everywhere for a very long time.

Watch for coronas when you are traveling in an automobile on a rainy or foggy night. The tiny droplets on the windshield scatter the light from oncoming cars and sometimes produce beautiful effects.

If you live where it is very cold in the winter, you may sometimes have moisture from your breath freeze on the windshield before the heater warms the interior of the car. This thin film of ice crystals produces haloes which are very brilliant.

CHAPTER 17

HAVE YOU NOTICED?

THERE ARE almost infinite possibilities in experimenting with light. If you have found the subject interesting, follow it further on your own. Here are some phenomena connected with light. You have probably noticed them and have formed a hypothesis about why each one works. How will you test it?

1. Many people are quite amazed in the springtime when they look out of their windows, for the stars seem to be centers of crosses in the sky. During the winter there were no crosses.

In the springtime we put screens on the windows. The screening serves to catch light, and each strand reflects it to our eye. The crosslike formation is produced on the screen itself. During the winter the screens were removed, and so no crosses were observed.

2. When we move, the moon appears to move with us. When we stop, the moon stops.

The moon is far away from us and so the angle at which we view the moon does not alter very much as we change position. We imagine it moves with us because we view it constantly at the same, or substantially the same, angle.

3. The reflection of a street lamp in a puddle at night when it is raining appears to be surrounded by sparks. The sparks all move away from the reflection of the lamp in straight lines.

Each drop sets up ripples which catch the light of the lamp. The light travels along so rapidly that we think we are seeing a streak of light; a spark.

4. Have you ever stood 10 feet or so from an ornamental garden mirror globe with the reflection of the sun covered by the shadow of your head? How does the sky look?

In a garden globe we can see the entire surface of the sky and earth confined in a circle. Of course the images are distorted. When standing so that your head covers the reflection of the sun, you can see haloes, rings, and also brightly colored clouds. In fact, you can see the entire sky, and the clouds and colors appear bright and colorful.

5. The spots of sunlight seen on the ground under trees are always perfectly circular. But the chinks between the leaves are all sorts of shapes.

The sun is not a mere pinpoint of light. It is a large source. Any opening in the leaves, therefore, produces many images of the sun. If you catch one of the light images on a piece of paper and raise the paper, you will find that the image becomes smaller. The light is therefore cone-shaped, showing it is produced by many points of light—the sun. The greater the distance of the ground from the opening between the leaves, the larger the spot of light.

6. Automobiles at a great distance are too small to be seen, but, if the sun hits their windshields at the proper angle, the light flashes and we can locate the position of the car.

The flash of light is very brilliant because the windshield concentrates a great deal of light into a small area. We can see this concentrated light, though we cannot see the diffused light coming from the car itself.

7. Grass with dew on it appears gray. If we examine a few blades of grass carefully, though, we will find that the droplets of dew are all clear and transparent.

Dew does not wet the grass; there is a layer of air between the drop and the blade itself. The gray appearance is caused by the reflection of light both inside and outside the droplet. When the drops are large, they are silvery because most of the light coming to us is reflected from the flat, back surface.

8. Perhaps you have heard people say that one could see the stars in the daytime if he went down in a deep well. Is this true or not?

There is no place where this condition has been observed. Some people have suggested that the stars could be seen if they were viewed through a narrow tube about 40 feet long. The effect, if true, would be due to the fact that side light which might dazzle vision is removed. But the field viewed by the observer—the sky—is still illuminated, and so the starlight would blend into the sky.

9. When you sit in a restaurant between parallel mirrors, several images of light at your table can be seen. They seem to disappear over a horizon, getting dimmer and dimmer as they go.

When images are seen in parallel mirrors, the image is reflected over and over again. The second mirror reflects to the first mirror; from here back to the second mirror, and so on.

10. Are all snowflakes white? Look at snow falling from a gray sky. Some of the flakes appear black.

Black, white, and gray differ only in brightness, and the background is the only standard of comparison. When snow falls, we use the sky as a background. Parts of the sky are definitely brighter than the snowflakes, therefore some of the flakes appear dark.

11. The two surfaces of ordinary window glass are not completely parallel. Have you observed how objects seen through some windows appear to stretch as if they were made of rubber as you move your head from side to side?

We see distortions from the curves in the glass. Sometimes the curves enlarge the image, or parts of it; at other times the curve makes the image smaller.

12. When you are awakened at night and first look at a light, a corona, or bright ring of light, appears about the bulb. This ring disappears quickly as our eyes become accustomed to the light.

The corona seems to be formed in the outer part of the lens. When your eyes are dark-adapted, the pupil is wide open, exposing the edge of the lens. When first you look at a light, therefore, you see the corona. Soon your iris closes, reducing the size of the pupil and covering the edge of the lens. The corona is no longer visible.

13. The lighted path across the water from the setting sun or rising moon seems to end at a distance from the shore on which you stand. Yet it would seem that the

sun or moon light must come all the way to the shore.

The sunlight and moonlight reflected by water forms a broad or a narrow column, depending on the height of the sun or moon and the roughness of the sea. The column is brightest near the horizon. As the sun or moon changes position, we view the light at a changing angle, and the angle limiting visibility is reached beyond the shore itself.

There are hundreds of aspects of light which are never noticed by most people. Keep on the alert for the odd and interesting appearances all around you. You will take great satisfaction from your experiments and observations of light.

INDEX

Nelson F. Beeler, coauthor with Dr. Branley of numerous science experiment books, was born in Adams, Massachusetts, and now lives in Potsdam, New York. Before becoming a professor at Potsdam State Teachers College, a unit of the State University of New York, he taught at Clarkson College and in high schools. He was head of the science department at the high school in Nyack, New York, and is a former president of the New York State Science Teachers Association. He holds degrees from the University of Massachusetts and Columbia University. For his doctorate, which he got at New York University, he studied children's science books from 1800.

Franklyn M. Branley, who lives in Westwood, New Jersey, is Associate Astronomer at the American Museum–Hayden Planetarium. He has taught at the Jersey City State Teachers College in Jersey City, New Jersey; at the State Teachers College in Troy, Alabama; and at Columbia University. Dr. Branley was born in New Rochelle, New York; was trained for teaching at the State Teachers College, New Paltz, New York; and holds degrees from New York University and Columbia University.